Red & Yellow's
Bright Ideas

Click. Create. Celebrate!™

Welcome to Our Bright Ideas Holiday Book!

Baking Tip: If directions say 20 minutes at 250°, don't try 10 minutes at 500°.

And CERTAINLY don't try 5 minutes at 1,000°.

Red: Yellow, keep mixing the dough! We have to finish the cookies for Santa! Ummm, tasty. . . . We know you love to spend time and have fun with your family and loved ones all year round, especially during holidays.

Yellow: We like spending time together too, right, Red?

Red: Stop interrupting, Yellow! That's why we've compiled this book full of fun activities and recipes for the holidays that will keep everybody busy doing interesting and creative things. We have Bright Ideas for just about every season and occasion: from delicious peanut butter cookies for Christmas to Valentine's Day gifts for classmates to games for summer rainy days—we have it all!

We hope you'll use these ideas as a starting point to invent family traditions of your own, like those of the families featured in each section. Why not read about how different families celebrate the holidays while you wait for a recipe to finish baking?

You did check the cookies in the oven, didn't you, Yellow?!?

Red & Yellow: We hope our Holiday Book helps you and your family make the time you spend together more special and more fun than ever. And you just might create some Bright Ideas of your own!

Signed,

RED! Yellow

P.S.: For more recipes, craft ideas and, of course, a picture of us, visit **marsbrightideas.com**.

BRIGHT IDEAS FOR

Lots of good recipes and ideas to keep families

happy and busy at holiday or special-occasion time.

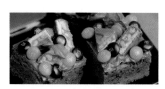

CHRISTMAS

Sophia's Perfect Cookies

NANCY HOLYOKE

 Reading Time 9–15 minutes

A girl in Iowa gets an important boost from a new neighbor in the nick of time.

"Please," Sophia said between clenched teeth. "Will you all just get out!" Tyler, who was 13, was sitting on the kitchen counter with his hand-held game station, drumming his feet against the dishwasher. Jenny, her little sister, was smushing sliced bananas into her plate with a fork. The twins, Matt and Jake, Sophia's cousins from Omaha, were having a sword fight in their underwear. They were three and going through a stage where they didn't like clothes. They said clothes felt "prickly." They didn't care that it was the day before Christmas, or that it was five below and snowing hard. They liked just underwear—and plastic helmets, plastic shields and plastic swords they could wave in the air.

"Ah-ha!" yelled Matt. He had the good sword; Jake's drooped at the handle.

"Ha!" yelled Jake.

"That is so cheap," muttered Tyler, who liked to talk to his games. He was

M&M'S® Chocolate Candies Peanut Butter Dippers

Makes 2 dozen dippers.

1 batch peanut butter cookie dough
Assorted holiday cookie cutters
2 bags **DOVE® Brand Milk or Dark Chocolate Gifts**
1½ feet wax paper
1 bag **M&M'S® Brand Milk Chocolate Candies for the Holidays**

1. Prepare cookie dough according to package or favorite recipe directions.
2. On a generously floured surface, roll dough to about ¼-inch thickness.
3. Using assorted holiday cookie cutters, cut out shapes, place on a nonstick baking sheet and bake according to recipe directions.
4. Let cookies cool on a wire rack.
5. Unwrap the DOVE® Chocolate Gifts into a microwave-safe bowl and melt in the microwave for 90 seconds, stirring occasionally, until smooth.
6. Dip cookies in the melted DOVE® Chocolate Gifts and place on wax paper.
7. Decorate with M&M'S® Chocolate Candies.
8. Let chocolate set before eating these holiday treats!

CHRISTMAS

Snowflakes

Can you catch snowflakes
on your tongue?
Here they come—one,
two, a slew of them
swirling from the sky.
They're sticking
To my eyelashes, my
scarf, my hat. If I stand
absolutely still,
snowflakes cover me until
I'm just a pile of white—
a snowflake man on the lawn,
I don't move, don't yawn
'til I hear bells jingle on a
sleigh—
Santa's coming!
"Step right this way"
is what my snowflake
man will say.

Holiday Time Turtles

Makes 2 dozen turtles.

1 bag **MILKY WAY**® Brand Miniatures,
unwrapped and roughly chopped
$^2/_3$ cup ($^1/_2$ 14-ounce can)
sweetened condensed milk
1 stick butter or margarine
2 cups shelled pecan pieces
1 bag **DOVE**® Brand Dark Chocolate
Gifts, unwrapped

1. Melt the MILKY WAY® Miniatures, condensed milk and butter in the top half of
a double boiler. Blend until smooth.
2. Remove from heat and add nuts.
Refrigerate for 20 minutes.
3. Drop by spoonfuls onto wax paper.
Freeze for 15 minutes.
4. Chop the DOVE® Chocolate Gifts. Melt
$^2/_3$ of the chocolate in the top half of a
double boiler. Once melted, remove
immediately from heat and add the
remaining chocolate. Stir until all the
chocolate has melted.
5. Using a fork, dip the MILKY WAY® mixture in the chocolate, one piece at a time.
6. Place turtles on a tray lined with
wax paper and freeze until firm, about
30 minutes.

Paper Cone Ornaments

Add something special to your tree trimming this year with these delightfully festive, easy-to-make ornaments.

Old Christmas cards   **Hole punch**
Double-stick tape   **Thin red ribbon**
1 bag M&M'S® Brand Milk Chocolate
   Candies for the Holidays

1. Make small paper cones out of old Christmas cards by wrapping the sides of the card around each other so the bottom is a point and the top is wide.
2. Double-stick tape the ends of the paper so you have a strong cone.
3. Punch a hole into each side of the cone and tape the ribbon with clear tape to the inside of the cone.
4. Fill with M&M'S® Chocolate Candies and hang as a decoration.

in seventh grade. Sophia was in fifth. Next year they'd be in the same school again and ride the same bus.

"Out! Out! I'm cooking!" Sophia cried. Nobody looked at her. From the basement came the sound of TV and more Lundberg relations.

The voice of Sophia's favorite uncle, Tim, came from the den. He was here from New York City for Christmas with his black beard and baseball cap, and was telling Sophia's father about running into their neighbor, Mrs. Sanchez, on the street in New York. It was amazing, said Uncle Tim. All those millions of people, and here was somebody from home coming toward him. You couldn't get away from Boyne, Iowa. It was a small world.

Sophia agreed. It was particularly small in this kitchen. "Mom!" she yelled. Why

did it have to be so cold out? The tradition was that everybody would be sledding now. They would come pouring back into the house just as Sophia was taking the cookies out of the oven. Her father would start the fire (also tradition) and everyone would have cookies and hot cocoa (buried in marshmallows—tradition).

"What great cookies!" they would say.

And nobody knew how to make them but Sophia. She loved being in charge of the kitchen for those few hours, rolling out her dough, smelling butter and flour. It was her favorite part of the holiday. It was her favorite part of the year. Her mother was often there, too, puttering around. They'd play Christmas music. Sophia made sure to chill the dough for just the right amount of time—if it was too cold you couldn't roll it; if it was too

CHRISTMAS

Surprise Balls

It's as much fun making a surprise ball for someone as it is getting to open one. A surprise ball is a bunch of little gifts wrapped up one by one in layers of any kind of paper, then wrapped all together in paper or felt. The gifts have to be little. Coins, key chains, necklaces, toy soldiers, bracelets, stickers, candy all work well. Just think small. (And funny!) And with felt and glue you can make a finished ball into a face or a creature.

For a great new Christmas tradition, have everyone in the family make a surprise ball for one other person who'll be at dinner. Draw names from a hat weeks before. (Keep the results secret!) If you draw your sister's name, include that bracelet she always admired. If you get Grandpa's name and he loves chocolate-chip cookies, hide a bag in the dishwasher and wrap up a clue telling him where to look.

It's Christmas Eve and in the dining room are creatures the size of softballs at every place. A frog here, an orc there. A reindeer, a cat, a cartoon character. What's going on? Surprise balls.

Santa's Surprise Cookies

These special cookies have a secret! Here's a hint: SNICKERS® fans will love them! Makes 2 dozen cookies.

2 sticks butter, softened
1 cup creamy peanut butter
1 cup light brown sugar
1 cup sugar
2 eggs
1 teaspoon vanilla extract
$3\frac{1}{2}$ cups sifted all-purpose flour
1 teaspoon baking soda
$\frac{1}{2}$ teaspoon salt
1 bag SNICKERS® Brand Miniatures, unwrapped
Powdered sugar
1 bag DOVE® Brand Milk or Dark Chocolate Gifts

1. Preheat the oven to 325°F.
2. Combine the butter, peanut butter and sugars using a mixer on a medium to low speed until light and fluffy.
3. Slowly add eggs and vanilla until thoroughly combined. Mix in flour, baking soda and salt.
4. Cover and chill dough for 2–3 hours.
5. Remove dough from refrigerator. Divide into 1-tablespoon pieces and flatten each.
6. Place a SNICKERS® Miniatures candy in the center of each piece of dough.
7. Form the dough into a ball around each SNICKERS® Miniatures candy.
8. Place on a greased cookie sheet and bake for 10–12 minutes. (Baking time and temperature may vary if using more than 1 tablespoon of dough per cookie.)
9. Sprinkle with powdered sugar, melt DOVE® Chocolate Gifts and drizzle on top.
10. Let cookies cool on rack or wax paper.

Silent Night Cupcakes

They'll light up your table or sweeten your holiday party! Makes 18 cupcakes.

- 1 bag **MILKY WAY® Brand Chocolate Covered Caramels**
- 1 box chocolate or white cake mix
- **Cupcake liners**
- 1 (16-ounce) container white frosting
- **Food coloring (optional)**
- 1 bag **M&M'S® Brand Peanut Chocolate Candies for the Holidays**
- 1 bag **M&M'S® Brand MINIS® Milk Chocolate Candies (optional)**

1. Set aside 18 MILKY WAY® Caramels. Chop the remaining MILKY WAY® Caramels and set aside.
2. Prepare the cake mix according to the package directions. Add the chopped candy to the batter.
3. Place the cupcake liners in cupcake pans, add the batter and bake according to directions.
4. Once baked, remove the cupcakes from the pan and allow to cool completely.
5. If desired, color frosting or use white frosting to ice the top of each cupcake. Press one reserved MILKY WAY® Caramels, standing straight up, into the center of the cupcake.
6. Using a dab of frosting, place a red M&M'S® Peanut Chocolate Candy straight up (like a flame), on top of the MILKY WAY® Caramels.
7. Optional: Sprinkle M&M'S® MINIS® Candies on top of the cupcake.

warm it stuck to the rolling pin. Then she'd cut cookies thinking about how proud she would feel when they came out perfectly, and about all the other perfect moments that lay ahead—about the dinner her mother would make, about the stories Uncle Tim would tell, about settling in between the sheets in a clean nightgown—

"That is so cheap!" Tyler cried.

"You can do that somewhere else," Sophia hissed.

"I don't want to do it somewhere else." His eyes didn't leave the screen.

"Mom!" Sophia was practically in tears. "The dough's ready to roll now!"

With relief, Sophia heard her mother's feet padding down the stairs. Like the twins, Mrs. Lundberg was often barefoot. She could walk the gravel drive to the mailbox in summer or winter. Sophia didn't

A Cool Rolling Pin

To keep butter-cookie dough
cool when you roll it out,
you need a chilled rolling pin.
Use one made of marble,
or make one: Remove the
paper label from a glass soda
bottle or cylindrical condi-
ments jar, fill it with ice
water, cap tightly and dry it
well. Use as a rolling pin.

just love her mother; she admired her.
Mrs. Lundberg was duly elected city-
councilperson for the ninth ward.
She might even run for mayor. If that
wasn't enough, she had Uncle Tim as
a brother—the coolest uncle in all
Iowa. Uncle Tim could draw. People
in New York paid him to do illustra-
tions. "Are you making your cookies
this year, I hope?" he had said. "It's

Fudge Crispy Truffles

Makes 40 truffles.

1 bag 3 **MUSKETEERS**® Brand Miniatures,
  unwrapped
2 tablespoons milk
2$\frac{1}{2}$ cups puffed cocoa cereal
Parchment or wax paper
3 tablespoons finely chopped walnuts
  or pecans (optional)
3 tablespoons confectioners'
  sugar (optional)

1. Roughly chop the 3 MUSKETEERS® Miniatures.
   In a heavy-bottomed pan, melt candy with milk,
   stirring constantly until smooth. Once melted,
   remove from heat immediately.
2. Stir in puffed cocoa cereal, mixing thoroughly.
   Drop by teaspoonfuls onto parchment-lined
   cookie sheets, making 40 mounds.
3. Cool 5–10 minutes, or until cool enough
   to handle.
4. With buttered fingers, roll mounds into
   1-inch balls.
5. If desired, roll balls in chopped nuts and/or
   confectioners' sugar, or simply leave them plain.

not Christmas without cookies."

And Tyler was sitting on the counter!

"OK, Ty," said Mrs. Lundberg. "Out you go."

"What?" said Tyler, as if this were the biggest betrayal since Anakin Skywalker went to the Dark Side.

"Sophia needs the counter. Boys, Jen, come on."

"I'm not touching her lousy cookies."

Sophia glared. "My cookies are perfect. They're a tradition."

Tyler rolled his eyes. "Oh, a tradition. Unlike Mrs. Sanchez's pinecone thing."

Sophia froze.

"What?" said Mrs. Lundberg.

"Sophia hid it, right, Soph? Because it wasn't tradition."

"Is that true?"

"I didn't hide it!"

"It" had been on the doorstep when they got back from Omaha after Thanksgiving. Mrs. Lundberg thought it might be a Santa. Sophia guessed it was a bear. Bears didn't have anything to do with Christmas. Anyway, Sophia didn't see why they had to move the reindeer that always sat on the dining-room shelf just because a neighbor had given them a bunch of pinecones. All she had done was put the reindeer back in its place and put the pinecone creation—well, on the workbench by the furnace. If her mother hadn't noticed, what harm was there in it?

Mrs. Lundberg frowned. "Mrs. Sanchez is coming for dinner, Sophia. I want the . . . Santa or bear or whatever back where I had it by the time she gets here. It will make her feel

M&M'S® Holiday Brownies

A rich, colorful layered treat that the family can help decorate. Makes 24 brownies.

1 box brownie mix (for 13 x 9-inch baking pan)
1 bag M&M'S® Brand Milk Chocolate Candies for the Holidays
2 (8-ounce) packages cream cheese
$2/3$ cup sugar
$1/4$ cup heavy cream
2 eggs
$1/2$ teaspoon vanilla extract
$1 1/2$ cups whipped cream (optional)

1. Preheat the oven to 350°F.
2. Prepare the brownie mix according to the package directions.
3. Spoon batter into 13 x 9-inch baking pan, spreading evenly.
4. Cover batter with 1 cup of M&M'S® Chocolate Candies.
5. In another mixing bowl, thoroughly beat the cream cheese with the sugar. Slowly add the heavy cream, eggs and vanilla. Blend mixture until smooth, scraping down the sides of the bowl several times.
6. Evenly spoon the cream-cheese mixture over the brownie batter.
7. Bake for 50–60 minutes, or until a toothpick inserted into the center comes out almost clean.
8. Remove and cool completely.
9. Optional: Just before serving, top with a layer of whipped cream.
10. Cut into 2-inch squares.
11. Prior to serving, decorate with M&M'S® Chocolate Candies. Refrigerate any leftovers.

Christmas Cupcake Tree

Makes 29 cupcakes.

29 plain cupcake liners
1 box vanilla or chocolate cake mix
$^1/_2$ bag 3 MUSKETEERS® Brand Miniatures, unwrapped
  and finely chopped
2 (16-ounce) containers vanilla frosting
Green food coloring
3 bags red and green M&M'S® Brand Chocolate Candies
  for the Holidays, plus yellow M&M'S® Milk Chocolate Candies
29 festive cupcake liners
4 plates about 2 inches, 6 inches, 10 inches and 14 inches
3 (6-ounce) glasses
3 bags Holiday Miniatures such as SNICKERS® Brand,
  3 MUSKETEERS® Brand and TWIX® Brand

1. Preheat the oven to 350°F. Place the plain cupcake liners in cupcake pans.
2. Prepare the cake batter according to the package directions. Fold in the chopped
   3 MUSKETEERS® Miniatures.
3. Spoon $^1/_2$ cup of the batter into the cupcake pans. Bake for 19–20 minutes. Cool completely.
4. Tint the vanilla frosting green and frost the cupcakes.
5. Decorate 28 cupcakes with red and green M&M'S® Chocolate Candies and 1 cupcake with
   the yellow M&M'S® Chocolate Candies. Place the cupcakes in the festive liners.
6. Stack the plates in decreasing size. Lift the top three plates, center a glass on the bottom
   plate, center the top three plates on the glass. Lift the top two plates and center a glass on
   the plate beneath, and so on. Check to make sure the plates and glasses are well balanced.
7. Arrange the green and red cupcakes on the three bottom plates; place the yellow cupcake
   on top for the star.
8. Garnish the tree with wrapped Miniature candies.

good. It's her first holiday without Mr. Sanchez, remember." Mrs. Lundberg turned away.

The others trailed after her. Sophia followed, angry and ashamed, carrying a chair.

"What's that for?" said Mrs. Lundberg.

"To put against the door."

"Really, Sophia. You can't shut yourself up in here. It's Christmas. It's about being together."

"You can be together," Sophia said, tears coming to her eyes. "I'm making cookies."

Christmas Place Cards

This season, why not make special place cards for Christmas dinner? Get some thick construction paper, then let everybody pick their own color. Each sheet of paper can make four cards. Fold the paper into fourths and cut along the folds. Fold each rectangle either way you like to make a tent. Write each person's name on one face in pencil, then trace the name with glue and sprinkle the glue with colored sparkles. To add a shape, draw a pine tree or wreath on the back side using the fold as your base line. Cut out the shape with a knife except along the fold. To make sure the shape sits upright, tape a toothpick to the back across the fold. Decorate with glue and sparkles. Or paste on that person's favorite movie star or athlete or hero. You'll want to save these place cards to use next Christmas, too.

•   •   •

A disaster. That's what it was. Sophia couldn't believe it. Baking powder. It was right there. How could she have forgotten to put it in? It would be nice to blame Tyler, but he had still been in bed when she made the dough. She'd forgotten. Simple as that. The cookies were as flat as the fancy French pancakes Uncle Tim made for Christmas breakfast. The cookies were terrible.

Christmas Wreath

This beautiful symbol of the holiday is a delicious way to say "Merry Christmas."

1 1/2 tablespoons margarine
5 ounces marshmallows
Green food coloring
3 cups crisp rice cereal
1 (16-ounce) container vanilla frosting
2 pounds M&M'S® Brand Milk Chocolate Candies for the Holidays
1 red satin bow

1. Melt margarine in a saucepan over low heat. Add marshmallows and stir until completely melted. Remove from heat and tint with food coloring. Mix in crisp rice cereal.
2. Coat your hands with margarine and form mixture into a ring on wax paper. (Ring should be about 7 inches in diameter.)
3. Stir a few drops of food coloring into the frosting until blended thoroughly. Reserve 1/4 cup and set aside. Using a butter knife or spatula, spread a thin layer of frosting over the entire ring.
4. Completely cover the ring with green M&M'S® Chocolate Candies. For any open spots, dab some of the vanilla frosting onto the backs of green M&M'S® Chocolate Candies and place where needed.
5. Dab frosting onto the red M&M'S® Chocolate Candies and place 3 candies in a cluster to create berries. Dab frosting onto the back of the bow and place on wreath. Slice to serve.

Teary again, Sophia was scraping cookie dough into the garbage when she heard a noise.

Tap-tap-tap. Was it Tyler, come to sneer at the mess? No, there was someone at the back

door. Or at least there was an enormous hooded parka with a baking dish. Sophia couldn't see who was in it till she opened the door.

"Hello, Sophia," said Mrs. Sanchez, trailing snow as she stepped into the kitchen. "Well, I'm in a pickle."

Mrs. Sanchez was taller than Sophia's father. She was broader, too. She looked like she could play football. In her hands, the big glass baking pan looked like a candy dish.

"My oven's gone out," the woman said. "Would you folks have room for my beans?"

"I guess so," said Sophia, glum. Why didn't Mrs. Sanchez just use her microwave? "I was making cookies, but I wrecked them."

"Oh, my dear, I'm so sorry," said Mrs. Sanchez. But she sounded delighted. She inspected the cookies. "Baking powder?"

Sophia nodded.

"Well, let's start over!" Mrs. Sanchez said gaily.

"There's no time," Sophia said. "The dough has to chill. Anyway, I don't have enough butter."

"I've got butter," said the woman, as if this were a bigger coincidence than being in New York on a Mid-Iowa Handicraft League bus tour and running into Uncle Tim. "And we can put the dough on the porch. That will hurry it up."

We? thought Sophia. Tyler pushed into the room. "Hi, Mrs. Sanchez. Don't have a fit, Soph. I just want to get some potato chips."

Fat chance, Sophia thought. He was here to steal the first cookie (again—a tradition). He drifted toward the counter, eyes on the cookies. Then he stopped.

Holiday Poppers

Enjoy a family gift-wrapping session during the holidays. Makes 8 poppers.

2 (16 x 27-inch) sheets red tissue paper
2 (16 x 27-inch) sheets green tissue paper
Red curling ribbon
Green curling ribbon
Gold curling ribbon
8 (5-inch) paper tubes (either cut a paper towel tube in half or use a toilet tissue tube)
Selection of DOVE® Brand Milk or Dark Chocolate Gifts; SNICKERS®, MILKY WAY®, 3 MUSKETEERS® and TWIX® Brand Miniatures

1. Cut the tissue paper in half lengthwise. Cut 8 strands of each color of ribbon 15" long.
2. Fill the tubes with a selection of DOVE® Chocolate Gifts; SNICKERS®, MILKY WAY®, 3 MUSKETEERS® and TWIX® Miniatures.
3. Lay one sheet of tissue paper flat on a surface. Place the tube at one edge and roll the paper tightly around the tube. Tie the ribbon tightly at both ends of the tube.
4. Once all the tubes are wrapped and tied, arrange in an attractive presentation, such as the one pictured.

"They're—flat," he said.

"I wrecked them, OK?" Sophia said.

"Really?" Tyler said. "That's too bad." You could tell he meant it. "I was kind of looking forward to a cookie." He came over and peered at the dough in the garbage. "The stuff looks OK. You can't add water or something?"

"No, I can't add water."

"Be a hero, Tyler," said Mrs. Sanchez. "Run next door and get my butter. Sophia and I will make a new batch."

Sophia heaved herself onto a stool. Tyler looked from his sister to Mrs. Sanchez and back. He picked up a flattened cookie and sniffed. "I always kind of wanted to try making cookies."

"No!" said Sophia.

"Wonderful!" said Mrs. Sanchez. She took off her coat. She wore a flowered apron over her dress.

Afterward, Sophia could never quite figure out how Mrs. Sanchez pulled it off. One minute the kitchen was nothing but dirty bowls. The next they were setting new dough out onto the porch to cool.

"This weather's good for something," Mrs. Sanchez said. "I thought I'd go crazy over at my place, all cooped up."

The dough was still a bit sticky when they brought it in, but Sophia was so clever with a rolling pin that a chunk came up only once. "Oh, no," she said. Mrs. Sanchez peeled it off, pushed it back down and dusted it with flour. "They won't be as tender," she said, "but they'll still be cookies."

It was Tyler—Tyler!—who turned out to be best at getting the cookies off the board and onto the cookie sheets. "Who's the man?" he'd say, slipping another one off his knife.

Tyler got serious about the cookie cutters, too. "We don't have enough snowmen," he said. "We don't want to hurt the snowmen's feelings."

In an hour the first cookies were sitting on the counter. They bulged here and there. Some of the angels were

Cut Paper Snowflakes

Use a plate to draw a circle on thin paper—any size or color. The bigger the circle, the more details you can cut into it. First fold the circle in half—that makes "fold A." Then fold the half-moon in half again—making a big pie-wedge piece. The new fold is "fold B." Next, one at a time, fold back the two "A" folds toward the "B" fold—one on either side. You now have a cheesecake-wedge piece.

Cut off the pointed tip. Use fancy-cut craft scissors to cut a big V or a wiggly line or a zigzag along the curved edge. Cut little nicks and Vs and half-circles or whatever else you want all the way up both sides of the wedge. If you have a hole punch, use that, too.

P.S. Did you know you can take any size piece of paper and fold it in half only six times? A seventh time is impossible. Try it!

CHRISTMAS

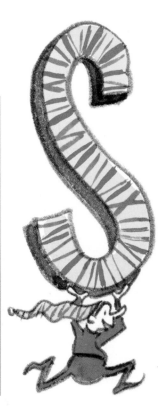

Willy-Nilly Winter Words

Put the letters in the right order and find a winter word. Have your family do one every day in December. The winner is declared after the last word is solved, the day after Christmas.

1. zeingerf
2. deguf
3. skeocoi
4. nesskaflow
5. yolhiad
6. reewtha
7. zraildbz
8. ogotnbag
9. ynarcbda
10. clieci
11. areonctoids
12. gepnniu
13. selovnigh
14. erssweat
15. leacchoot
16. oilgo
17. rapak
18. bonslawl
19. orfyst
20. ehvirs
21. bentsalk
22. neladcs
23. dregigce nrat
24. stefa
25. prempeptin
26. stinmet

Answers to Willy-Nilly Winter Words

1-freezing, 2-fudge, 3-cookies, 4-snowflakes, 5-holiday, 6-weather, 7-blizzard, 8-toboggan, 9-candybar, 10-icicle, 11-decorations, 12-penguin, 13-shoveling, 14-sweater, 15-chocolate, 16-igloo, 17-parka, 18-snowballs, 19-frosty, 20-shiver, 21-blankets, 22-candles, 23-greeting card, 24-feast, 25-peppermint, 26-mittens

stretched. And Tyler had got carried away with the sprinkles in places. But Mrs. Sanchez was right: They were still cookies.

"Here's to us," said Mrs. Sanchez. While she took another sheet from the oven, Sophia pulled Tyler aside and whispered in his ear. Tyler nodded and drifted down the basement steps.

As Sophia and Mrs. Sanchez arranged cooled cookies on plates, Mrs. Sanchez cleared her throat. "I have a confession to make, Sophia," she said. "My oven works fine. I just got lonely. I always used to bake for Mr. Sanchez on Christmas. I saw you over here through the window, and I just—well, I wanted to make cookies."

Out of the corner of her eye Sophia saw Tyler tiptoe up the basement steps and slink across the kitchen. "I'm glad you came," said Sophia, and as soon as she spoke, she realized it was true. She'd had fun. She could get used to having help with her cookies. "I was going to give up."

"I know that feeling," said Mrs. Sanchez, serious. Then she perked up again. "Well, let's feed the masses!"

In the dining room, Mrs. Sanchez stopped short, looking at the pile of pinecones on the shelf. "Oh!" she said.

"We love the . . . decoration you made

23

Felt Holly Napkin Rings

- Brown, red and green felt and hot glue
- Plain and decorative scissors

For each napkin ring, cut a brown felt strip 2 inches wide by 7 inches long using plain or decorative scissors. Cut two 2-inch-long holly leaves free-hand from green felt. Cut dot-sized circles for berries from red felt. Glue leaves and berries to the center of the band. To make the napkin ring, apply hot glue to one end of the brown strip. Make a circle, overlapping at least one inch onto the glued area. Variation: Glue real holly leaves and berries to each felt strip before making the band.

Shortbread Candy Canes

Easy to make, easy to decorate and fun to eat. Makes 20 candy canes.

1 cup butter, at room temperature
$1/2$ cup confectioners' sugar
$1^3/_4$ cups flour
$1/4$ teaspoon baking powder
$1/4$ teaspoon salt
1 (16-ounce) container white frosting
1 bag M&M'S® Brand Milk Chocolate Candies for the Holidays

1. Preheat the oven to 350°F.
2. Combine butter and confectioners' sugar.
3. Add flour, baking powder and salt.
4. Form dough and roll out on a floured surface, to about $1/4$-inch thickness.
5. Cut candy cane shapes with cookie cutter or knife.
6. Bake for about 10 minutes, or until light brown. Let cool.
7. Frost with white frosting and decorate with M&M'S® Chocolate Candies.

us," said Sophia behind her.

"You do?" Mrs. Sanchez screwed up her face. "I'm not sure it's a very successful turkey. But does your mother always leave the Thanksgiving decorations up through Christmas?"

Sophia blinked. "Yes," she said. "It's a tradition."

Then Uncle Tim was there. "Finally!" he said. He greeted Mrs. Sanchez while Jenny and the twins descended on the cookies. Uncle Tim took one, too. "You look familiar," he said, squinting at Sophia as if noticing her for the first time. "But it's been so long. . . ." Then to Mrs. Sanchez: "Did you have one of Sophia's cookies? They're great. She disappears for hours, and then comes out all alone with these cookies."

"I had help," Sophia said.

Uncle Tim pointed at her. "Now I remember. Aren't you from Boyne, Iowa?"

Sophia nodded. "Small world," she said. ∎

Valentine's Day

Valentines Are Read

PETER AND CONNIE ROOP

 Reading Time 11–16 minutes

An unexpected turn gives Victor a Valentine's Day to remember.

Victor scratched his arm. It had itched all afternoon. Now, after dinner, his stomach itched, too. He lifted his shirt. "Mom, what are these red spots on my stomach?" Victor asked.

"Those spots look like bug bites!" exclaimed six-year-old Valerie.

"Let me take a closer look," Mom said. She bent down and stared at Victor's stomach. She put her hand on his forehead.

"You feel hot, Victor," Mom said.

"Let me take your temperature," said Dad, as he went to get the thermometer.

"What's wrong with me?" asked Victor.

"I think you have the chicken pox," Mom told him.

Dad put the thermometer into Victor's mouth.

"Victor has the chicken pox, chicken feet and dirty socks," Valerie chanted.

With the thermometer in his mouth, Victor couldn't say a word.

"We won't know unless we find feathers on his pillow," Dad said, laughing.

Victor began to scratch his stomach, but Mom said, "Stop."

Brownie Hearts

Makes 8 individual cakes.

1 box yellow cake mix
1 (16-ounce) container white frosting
Red food coloring
1 bag M&M'S® Brand Milk Chocolate Candies for Valentine's Day
Heart-shaped cookie cutter
1 bag DOVE® Brand Milk or Dark Chocolate Hearts

1. Make cake according to package directions. Pour into a 13 x 9-inch pan and bake until done.
2. Allow to cool. Cut cake in half lengthwise.
3. Create pink frosting by placing white frosting in a bowl and adding red food coloring until desired shade of pink is achieved.
4. Spread frosting onto one layer of cake. Sprinkle with M&M'S® Chocolate Candies, then top with remaining layer of cake.
5. Using a heart-shaped cookie cutter, cut hearts out of cake and place onto wire rack.
6. To melt DOVE® Chocolate Hearts, microwave for approximately 3–4 minutes on medium power, stirring every 20–30 seconds, being careful not to burn.
7. Pour the melted DOVE® Chocolate Hearts over heart-shaped cakes, being sure to cover completely.
8. Decorate with M&M'S® Chocolate Candies as desired.

Valentine's Day

Dad took the thermometer out of Victor's mouth. "99.9 degrees," he announced. "Victor has a fever."

"You can't go to school tomorrow," Mom said.

"Why not?" asked Victor.

"You're contagious," Mom explained.

"What's contagious mean?" Valerie asked.

"It means he could give the chicken pox to everyone in his class."

"But I have to go to school tomorrow," Victor cried. "It's Valentine's Day and we're having a big party."

"Victor, if you went to school, they would send you right home," Dad said.

Victor had tears in his eyes. He had already signed all of his valentines for his class. He had a special one with flowers on it for Mrs. Loveall, his third grade teacher. He also had a cool one with space aliens on it for his friend Walker, the new boy who had just moved to North Dakota from California. And there was the very, very special one for Heidi. Suddenly, Victor had an idea.

"Can Valerie take my cards to school for me?" he asked.

"No," Dad said. "Valerie can't go to school either. She might be contagious, too."

Valerie burst into tears and ran to her room.

"I'll call Grandma and see if she can spend the day while we are at work," Mom said. Victor loved his grandmother. They had fun together making things. But he would miss the Valentine's party!

"Victor, I had chicken pox when I was your age," Dad said.

"I bet you didn't have to miss your Valentine's party!" Victor moaned.

Valentine Candy Cone

These candy-filled cones make a great gift for classrooms or any fun group. Makes 6 cones.

1 bag M&M'S® Brand Chocolate Candies for Valentine's Day

Plastic wrap

Tape

6 sugar cones

Red or pink cellophane, cut into six 10-inch squares

6 strands thin red or pink ribbon

1. Loosely wrap ½ cup of M&M'S® Chocolate Candies in plastic wrap and tape it closed.
2. Set some of the wrapped candy on top of a cone.
3. Cover the candy with cellophane and tie with a ribbon.
4. Repeat steps 1 through 3 to fill the remaining cones.

Valentine's Day

I Love Cheesecake

Makes 12 cakes.

12 large cupcake liners

Large cupcake pan

1 cup ground chocolate wafers

2 tablespoons butter, melted

3 (8-ounce) packages cream cheese, softened

$1/2$ cup sugar

3 large eggs

Resealable plastic bag

Red food coloring

1 bag M&M'S® Brand Chocolate Candies for Valentine's Day

1. Preheat the oven to 350°F. Place the cupcake liners in a large cupcake pan.
2. Combine ground wafers with melted butter. Spoon 1 tablespoon into the bottom of each cup. Press to make an even layer. Set aside.
3. In a large bowl, beat together the cream cheese and sugar. Add eggs, one at a time, beating well after each addition.
4. Spoon $1/2$ cup of the batter into the plastic bag. Set aside.
5. Tint the remaining cheesecake batter pink. Fold $1 1/2$ cups of M&M'S® Chocolate Candies into the tinted cheesecake batter. Spoon the batter into the prepared cups.
6. Snip a very small corner of the plastic bag with the plain batter. Pipe small dots on top of the tinted batter.
7. Bake until almost set, about 15–18 minutes. Transfer to a wire rack and cool in pan. Refrigerate for at least 1 hour. Dot cheesecakes with remaining M&M'S® Chocolate Candies.

Valentine Pockets

Valentines can have gifts inside. Make a Valentine Pocket out of red felt, using a paper template in a heart shape to guide you as you cut two good-sized felt hearts with scissors. Then stitch or glue the two hearts together at the edges, leaving the top open. Fill the heart with something really nice—candy, coins or slips of paper that say lovely things such as "Be my valentine" and "You're sweet" and "Free hug." A bigger Valentine Pocket makes a wonderful—and reusable—package for giving Dad a necktie or Mom a necklace.

"No," Dad said. "I had to miss the state soccer championship." Victor liked soccer and sort of knew how his dad must have felt. Mom came back into the kitchen.

"Grandma will be here at seven in the morning and can stay for supper. She said being with Victor and Valerie would be the best Valentine's present ever."

Before Victor went to sleep he put all of his valentines into a box and slid them under his bed.

Victor woke up in the morning to delicious smells coming from the kitchen. He hopped out of bed and ran down the hall. He gave Grandma a huge hug.

"I made your favorite breakfast, pancakes," Grandma said. Valerie was already at the table enjoying heart-shaped pink pancakes. All at once Victor remembered. It was Valentine's Day and he would miss the party at school!

"Victor, you look like you bit a sour lemon," said Grandma.

Valentine's Day Love Pops
Makes 10 pops.

1 (18-ounce) package refrigerated sugar cookie dough
Large heart-shaped cookie cutter
Lollipop sticks (in arts and crafts stores)
1 (16-ounce) container white frosting
Red food coloring
M&M'S® Brand Milk Chocolate Candies for Valentine's Day
DOVE® Brand Milk Chocolate Hearts, pink or red cellophane and curling ribbon (optional)

1. Preheat the oven to 350°F.
2. Roll the dough to $1/4$-inch thickness, cut into heart shapes and place on a nonstick baking sheet.
3. Press a lollipop stick into the bottom half of each cookie.
4. Bake for 12–14 minutes. Cool completely.
5. Tint the frosting to the desired shade of pink.
6. Frost the cookies and decorate with M&M'S® Chocolate Candies.
7. Optional: Adhere two DOVE® Chocolate Hearts to cookie center with frosting. Wrap cookies with squares of cellophane and tie with ribbon.

Valentine Rebus Vocabulary

Rebus puzzles or stories mix pictures or symbols, words and combinations of letters and numbers that sound like a syllable of a word (such as the number "8" for the sound "ate"). To combine a letter and a picture, put a plus sign (+) in between. For example, a "T" plus a picture of a chicken (hen) makes "THEN" and a ♥ means "LOVE." Can you guess the rebus riddle at left? (BE MINE.) Use rebuses for valentines or in your diary to help keep things secret!

Victor tried to smile. There was nothing he could do, so he might as well make the most of a day off from school. He'd watch TV, play computer games, maybe even work on his airplane model.

Valerie piped up. "Victor, you won't believe all that we are going to do with Grandma. We are going to bake sugar cookies with red candies, make valentines for Mom and Dad, make peppermint candy, bake a cake and . . ." She stopped to pop a piece of pancake into her mouth.

Victor frowned as he considered these new plans for his day off from school.

"The first one who can tell me who St. Valentine was gets to lick the cookie dough spoon," Grandma said.

❤❤❤❤❤❤❤❤❤❤
Promises to Keep

A valentine card that says "I love you" is really nice, but why not a card that gives something, too—something only you can give? Like chores and pleasures for free: one car wash, one errand, one dog walk, one cleaned-up room. Give what your valentine really wants from you!

Peanut Lovers' Dream Bar
Makes 12 bars.

2 cups graham cracker crumbs

$1/4$ cup sugar

6 tablespoons butter, melted

I bag DOVE® Brand Chocolate Hearts, melted

2 cups chopped SNICKERS® Brand Miniatures

$1/2$ cup butter

$1/2$ cup chunky peanut butter

$1/2$ cup sugar

$1/2$ cup brown sugar

I egg

$1/2$ teaspoon vanilla extract

$1 1/4$ cups flour

I teaspoon baking soda

$1/2$ cup melted caramel squares (available in the candy aisle of a grocery store), or use caramel ice cream topping

1. Preheat the oven to 350°F.
2. Toss together the first 3 ingredients and press into bottom of 12 x 8-inch pan sprayed with cooking spray. Bake for about 10 minutes, or until firm.
3. Spread DOVE® chocolate over graham cracker crust, sprinkle with half of the SNICKERS® Miniatures. Place in refrigerator for about 15 minutes, or until the chocolate is set.
4. Cream butter, peanut butter, sugars, egg and vanilla together in a mixer. Add flour and baking soda. Spread over chocolate SNICKERS® Miniatures layer and bake 20–25 minutes longer, or until light brown.
5. Drizzle caramel on top and scatter remaining SNICKERS® Miniatures, pressing to adhere to caramel.

Valentine's Day

M&M'S® Crispy Hearts

Makes 1 large heart, 12–15 small hearts.

1 (10-ounce) bag large marshmallows
3 tablespoons butter
6 cups crispy rice cereal
Medium heart-shaped cake pan or heart-shaped cookie cutters and baking pan
Nonstick spray
1 (16-ounce) container white frosting
2 bags M&M'S® Brand Milk Chocolate Candies for Valentine's Day

1. Mix the marshmallows and butter in a microwave bowl. Cover the bowl with a piece of plastic wrap. Poke several holes into the plastic wrap. Microwave for 2 minutes, or until melted. Add the cereal and blend.
2. To make one large heart: Spray the cake pan with a nonstick spray. Add the cereal mixture and press it firmly into the corners of the pan. Cool for 20 minutes. To decorate: Unmold the heart and set it in the center of a plate. Spread the top of the heart with the frosting, leaving a $1/_2$-inch rim around the edges. Make a single layer of M&M'S® Chocolate Candies on top of the frosting.
3. To make small hearts: Press the mixture evenly into a baking pan coated with a nonstick spray. Using a heart-shaped cookie cutter (any size), press out cookie hearts. Decorate the cookies by first spreading them with white or tinted frosting. Then cover the surface with M&M'S® Chocolate Candies.

Heart-Shaped Pancakes

These are the perfect thing to serve Valentine's Day morning. You and Mom need a large heart-shaped cookie cutter and a blender to puree added ingredients. Use a favorite pancake recipe or add a beaten egg to fluff up pancake mix. For pink color and sweet flavor, blend thawed frozen strawberries or pitted cherries with the liquid the recipe calls for. Place the metal cookie cutter on a hot griddle before pouring batter. Be sure to use an oven mitt to move the cookie cutter! Serve with raspberry sauce or strawberry syrup.

Valentine's Day

Victor answered quickly. "He lived a long time ago and was put in jail for talking about the king. He fell in love with the jailer's blind daughter and wrote her love letters signed 'From Your Valentine.'"

Grandma smiled and said, "That's why today we send valentines to people we love." She dipped her wooden spoon into the cookie dough. She handed the spoon to Victor. A big glob of dough with red candies fell onto his plate.

Valerie smacked her lips as Victor licked the spoon. "What did the girl octopus say to the boy octopus?" Grandma asked.

"I want to hold your hand, hand, hand, hand, hand, hand, hand, hand!" Valerie shouted. Grandma handed her another spoon dripping with cookie dough.

Victor and Valerie helped Grandma do the dishes. When they were finished, Grandma set a big basket on the table. She pulled out ribbons, lace, paper and old valentine cards. "Making valentines by hand is an old tradition," Grandma explained. "We can each make cards for the people we love."

Valerie got the scissors. Victor brought some glue. Grandma sorted through the ribbons, lace and paper. "I remember the first valentine your grandpa gave me," Grandma said. "It was on red paper and had a big lace heart on the front. He made it himself, just like we are doing."

"That's what I'll make for you, Grandma," Valerie said. She struggled to cut a heart out of lace.

"Let me show you something Mrs. Loveall taught us," Victor offered. He took a square piece of paper, folded it in half and cut half a heart. When he unfolded the paper, he had a heart. Valerie copied Victor and the next heart

Love Coins

Make your own money for Valentine's Day! Smooth a sheet of heavy aluminum foil on several layers of newspaper. Make a series of coin shapes by placing a glass rim onto the foil and turning to mark circles. Use a ballpoint pen to gently emboss coin designs. Words have to be mirror images. Spell "love money" like this: YƎNOM ƎVO⅃. To give coins a firm backing, hot-glue red cardboard to the sheet of tokens, then cut them out. Give to family and friends for them to "spend."

she cut was perfect.

While Valerie made her card, Victor made a pop-up one with a bouncing heart in the middle for Mom. He made another for Dad shaped like a soccer ball. The kitchen filled with the delicious smell of cookies baking. Victor was enjoying himself so much that he even forgot about the party at school. He looked at Valerie's second card trimmed with lace and red ribbons. On the inside she had written, "TE AMO, PAPA."

"What does TE AMO, PAPA mean?" Grandma asked.

Valerie smiled. "You mean you don't know, Grandma?" Valerie asked. Grandma shook her head.

"I am learning Spanish at school. TE AMO, PAPA means I LOVE YOU, DADDY in Spanish!" Valerie exclaimed.

"Well, TE AMO, VALERIE AND VICTOR!" Grandma said, laughing, as she gave each of them a kiss and took the cookies out of the oven. While the cookies cooled, Victor had an idea. He ran to his room and came back with his box of valentines for school. He put them onto the table and began opening them.

"What are you doing?" Valerie asked. "You are supposed to give them away, not keep them yourself."

"Since I can't go to school and give the cards to my friends, I will send them on the computer."

"How can you send your cards on the computer?" Grandma asked.

"It's easy," Victor told her. "You

Chocolate Mousse
Makes 2 servings.

- **I bag DOVE® Brand Milk or Dark Chocolate Hearts**
- **2 cups whipping cream**
- **3 tablespoons sugar**
- **I teaspoon pure vanilla extract (or other pure extract such as orange or almond)**

1. Place 50 DOVE® Chocolate Hearts in a heatproof bowl.
2. Heat I cup whipping cream until hot but not boiling.
3. Pour cream over chocolate and stir until chocolate is completely melted.
4. Cool to room temperature. Whip remaining cup of cream with sugar and vanilla or other extract until fluffy, with soft peaks.
5. Gently fold into cooled chocolate until well blended.
6. Pour into individual parfait glasses or cups and chill at least 2 hours, preferably overnight.
7. Before serving, decorate each dessert cup with a dollop of whipped cream and one or two unwrapped DOVE® Chocolate Hearts.

Amo Liebe Amore Amour

Using dictionaries, the library, the Internet, the telephone and friends, see in how many languages you can write "I love you," then make a valentine using a different handwriting style or typeface for each "I love you."

just use a scanner. Dad showed me how."

"Can I do it, too?" begged Valerie.

"Sure," Victor said.

Valerie went to get her cards. Soon the kitchen table was piled with cards and empty envelopes. Victor turned on the computer. He typed in Mrs. Loveall's school e-mail address and wrote, "Roses are red. Victor is, too. Pick out a valentine from me to you!"

He placed his cards upside down on the scanner one by one and scanned them into the computer. He numbered the images and put them into a folder he labeled VicVal. Then he sent his valentine file to his class. Victor showed Valerie how to send her cards to her class. Grandma helped Valerie type in her message. "Roses are red. Hearts are, too. Valerie is having fun. How about you?"

Valerie pushed the "send" button. Grandma laughed and said, "Well, I've seen many different kinds of valentines but never an electronic valentine! And now I think the cookies must be ready."

As they enjoyed their warm cookies Valerie asked, "Grandma, won't the cookies spoil our lunch?"

"No, darling. We still have pink peppermint candy to make before I can fix lunch. This afternoon, I will need you and Victor to help me make our surprise Valentine's dinner for your parents."

"It's a special Valentine's Day, Valerie," Victor said. "Thank you, Grandma, for the best Valentine's Day ever."

Pink Mousse Tart

Makes 1 tart.

Heart-shaped 9-inch pan
Wax paper
1 package refrigerated brownie dough
1 bag MILKY WAY® Brand Miniatures
2 cups prepared vanilla pudding
3 tablespoons raspberry jam
Red food coloring
1 ¹/₂ cups whipped topping or whipped cream
1 bag DOVE® Brand Dark Chocolate Hearts
Resealable plastic bag

1. Preheat the oven to 350°F.
2. Line the bottom of a heart-shaped pan with wax paper. Press the brownie mixture into the bottom of the pan. Bake according to package directions until just cooked. Remove the brownie from the pan and place on a wire rack to cool for 10 minutes. Transfer the brownie to a flat serving plate.
3. While warm, press the MILKY WAY® Miniatures, side by side, around the entire rim of the heart. Let the brownie cool completely.
4. In a medium bowl, whisk together pudding and raspberry jam until smooth. Tint it with a few drops of red food coloring until bright pink. Fold in the whipped topping until just combined.
5. Spoon raspberry mousse into cooled tart.
6. Melt 8 DOVE® Chocolate Hearts in a microwave and pour into a resealable plastic bag. Make a very small snip in a corner of the bag and drizzle the chocolate over the mousse. Refrigerate until ready to serve.

Valentine's Day

Friendship Butterflies

Makes I butterfly.

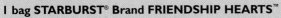

I (4-inch) cardboard tube
Purple tissue paper
Double-stick tape
Brightly colored construction paper
Chenille pipe cleaners
I bag STARBURST® Brand FRIENDSHIP HEARTS™
I bag M&M'S® Brand Chocolate Candies for Valentine's Day

1. Cover the cardboard tube with purple tissue paper, securing it with tape. Fold the ends of the paper inside the tube.
2. Make the butterfly wings by cutting 6 hearts (2 each of 3 different sizes) from construction paper. According to size, from the largest to the smallest, use double-stick tape to adhere the 3 hearts together. Repeat for the other set of 3 hearts. Attach the wings to the tube.
3. Cut two 2-inch circles from construction paper. Tape one circle to the front of the tube for the face and the second circle at the bottom of the tube. Tape the opening closed.
4. Bend a pipe cleaner into a V. Tape it onto the back of the butterfly "face" to make antennas.
5. Using double-stick tape, attach 8 STARBURST® FRIENDSHIP HEARTS™ down the tube for the "feet" and 2 hearts for the butterfly's eyes.
6. Fill the tube with M&M'S® Chocolate Candies and seal.

A Treat for a Friend

Everyone has a person or two nearby who don't get enough attention. Mid-February can be so cold and gray: Why not brighten their mood on Valentine's Day? Decorate a small paper bag with valentines cut from pink, red or white paper and glued on. Or draw valentines with crayons or markers. Then fill with slightly crushed pink, red or white tissue paper, on top of which you place wrapped Valentine candies and a card you have made that says "Be My Valentine!" It's best to drop off your valentine basket in person, if you can. Otherwise, be sure to seal it inside a bag or box and leave it in a secure place where your friend is sure to find it.

Adele's Easter Parade

ANDREA DiNOTO

 Reading Time 9–15 minutes

A country girl travels to the big city for a special Easter celebration.

Two fat robins were hopping around the backyard. The snow had all melted and the ground was mushy and wet. I saw one actually pull a worm out. Great worm weather! Where I live, in upstate New York, we call March the mud season. Oh, it's cold. But spring is coming. You can feel it.

Like every morning, I checked my e-mail. There was a message from my grandmother:

From: Gran
Subject: Bonnets
Darling Adele: How are you, sweetheart? Sunny and so windy here in the city I nearly got blown away when I went out for groceries this morning. Got all my apartment windows open—letting fresh air in. I'm thinking Easter hats. Better get busy, don't you think? Can you believe Easter's just a month away? We'll all meet at the parade as usual. Delly, I bet you can use your hat from last year. Just put on new things. What do you think? Lots of love. Gran.

Every year Grandma and I make Easter bonnets. We wear them in the

Easter Bonnets
Makes 10 bonnets.

1 package refrigerated sugar cookie dough or ten 4^1/$_2$-inch cookies

10 medium (2^1/$_2$-inch) cupcakes

2 (16-ounce) containers white frosting

Food coloring

M&M'S® Brand Milk Chocolate Candies for Easter, STARBURST® Brand Jellybeans, SKITTLES® Brand Bite Size Candies for Easter, STARBURST® FUN SIZE® Fruit Chews for Easter

1. Roll the sugar cookie dough to ^{1}/$_4$-inch thickness. Press out ten 4^1/$_2$-inch cookies. Bake according to the package directions. Set aside.
2. Remove the cupcake liners. Cut the top of each cupcake flat. Frost each with 1 tablespoon of frosting. Place the cupcakes upside down on the cookies. Set on a wire rack.
3. Divide the frosting into 4 bowls. Tint each bowl to a pastel shade. Place each bowl in the microwave for 15 seconds, then stir so it's easy to pour but not runny—like a milk shake. Spoon over the hats, completely covering them. Set aside for 10 minutes to firm.
4. Decorate using M&M'S® Chocolate Candies, STARBURST® Original Jellybeans and SKITTLES® Bite Size Candies.
5. To make hat ribbons, soften STARBURST® FUN SIZE® Fruit Chews in the microwave for 5 seconds. Then thinly roll them, cut them into ribbons and wrap them around the hats.

EASTER

famous parade on Fifth Avenue in New York City. It's totally fun. Everybody goes—Mom and Dad and my brother, Greg. He's ten. Two years younger than I am. After the parade, we go to Gran's apartment in Queens, which is one of the five boroughs of NYC, for a traditional Italian Easter dinner together. Grandma's an awesome cook, and she makes great Easter hats, too. She was right— Easter was coming soon. I'd better get busy. I hit "reply":

From: Adele
Subject: Re: Bonnets
OK. Will put my thinking bonnet on. Bunnies??? Eggs??? Hmmm. LUL (which means love you lots). Gotta go now. xxoo

I could hear Mom in the kitchen starting her "spring cleaning." What a racket! Pulling everything out of cupboards and giving the house a good scrubdown. "Getting rid of winter's ghosts," she calls it. I pulled on my jeans and boots.

"Mom," I said, "what kind of Easter hat should I make this year?"

"I don't know, Delly," she said, "but we've got egg dyeing to think of, too, and Easter baskets for the children at the hospital."

In spring, it's a local tradition for the Easter bunny—actually Mr. Hansen, a retired policeman dressed up in a rabbit costume—to visit the sick kids in the children's wing and take them baskets made by lots of the town people, including us.

"By the way," my mother said, "Carol Jameson just called to say she

Why Easter Eggs and Bunnies?

Spring's when nature awakens after a long winter's sleep. Since ancient times, the egg has symbolized this explosion of new life. Easter is actually named for Eastre (or Eostre or Ostara), the pagan goddess of spring, who was represented by the ancient Saxons as—would you believe?—a long-eared, egg-laying rabbit. Even egg dyeing dates to the second century, when colored eggs were exchanged as gifts.

The Most Gorgeous Eggs

Over a hundred years ago, a famous Russian jeweler made fabulous Easter eggs of gold and precious gemstones for the czars of Russia. Each gorgeous egg had a delightful surprise inside—like a tiny jeweled flower, a mechanical cuckoo, an elaborate miniature city scene or a watch. Have you heard of these eggs and this jeweler? To find out about them, go onto the Internet and type "Russian jeweled eggs" in the search window of your browser or any good search engine.

Egg Tree Topiary

Imagine this beautiful tree on your dinner table—or give it as a gift when you celebrate Easter! Makes 1 tree.

- 1 (14-inch) Styrofoam cone
- 1 piece colorful tissue paper
- Floral oasis (green Styrofoam material used in flower arranging and available in craft stores)
- 1 (5-inch) flowerpot
- 1 (10-inch) wooden dowel
- Double-stick tape
- 3 bags DOVE® Brand Milk or Dark Chocolate Eggs
- 1 bag M&M'S® Brand Speckled Milk Chocolate Eggs for Easter or STARBURST® Brand Jellybeans
- Pastel ribbon

1. Wrap the Styrofoam cone with tissue paper.
2. Cut the floral oasis to fit the flowerpot.
3. Press half the wooden dowel into the bottom of the Styrofoam cone. Set the rest of the dowel into the floral oasis–filled flowerpot, firmly securing the Styrofoam cone. Starting at the bottom and using double-stick tape, tape rows of DOVE® Chocolate Eggs in wrappers onto the cone.
4. Scatter the M&M'S® Speckled Eggs and STARBURST® Jellybeans around the base of the cone. Then tie a big bow of pastel ribbon around the flowerpot!

❀ spring poem ❀

mud is squishy between my toes, flowers bloom beneath my nose
birds are singing, bells are ringing
    the easter bunny hides eggs on the farm
      when I get close, mom yells, "you're warm!"
pollywogs squiggle in the creek (they'll be frogs within a week)
    it must be spring

found a puppy running loose over on Route 22 a few days ago. No one claimed her and Carol wants to find her a home. You and Greg and Daddy should go have a look." She said this like she meant it, too, which was a good sign.

"Really? You mean we could adopt her?"

"Why not?" she said. "As long as Pepper approves."

Pepper, our crazy cat, was sitting in the dining room window making those weird "keck-keck-keck" sounds at the birds in the yard.

I ran upstairs yelling at Greg, "Get dressed, fast. We're going with Dad to see a puppy and Mom says we can adopt her."

For once Greg was willing to drop his video game. While he put his shoes on I e-mailed Gran:

Easter Cupcakes

Sweet and speckled with jellybeans! These cupcakes bring spring fever to a delicious new level. Makes 24 cupcakes.

1 (18.25-ounce) box yellow cake mix
1 (16-ounce) container white frosting
Green food coloring (optional)
1 bag STARBURST® Brand Jellybeans

1. Make cupcakes according to the package directions.
2. If desired, tint the frosting with green food coloring to resemble grass.
3. Pipe or spread frosting onto the cooled cupcakes and place STARBURST® Jellybeans on top.

Sweet Carrots

Vegetables were never this much fun! Makes 4 carrots.

2 (14-inch) squares orange cellophane
Double-stick tape
1 bag M&M'S® Brand Milk Chocolate or Peanut Chocolate Candies
Green curling ribbon

1. Cut each cellophane square in half on the diagonal.
2. Using your thumb and forefinger, hold the middle of the cut diagonal edge of cellophane (the longest side). This middle point will become the tip of the cone.
3. Using your other hand, roll the cellophane around, keeping that middle point as the tip, and make the cone.
4. Tape both the inside and outside edges of the cone closed.
5. Fill the cone two-thirds full with the chosen candy.
6. Twist the top and tie it closed with the green ribbon.

To: Gran
Subject: Puppy
Guess what? A friend of Mom's found a lost puppy and Mom says we can adopt her. Keep your fingers crossed.

She was chocolate-colored, silky and shorthaired with floppy ears and big feet. Dad said, "She's got some Lab in her. She'll be big, for sure." Dad works for the electric company. He was glad to have the day off after working a zillion hours of overtime last week.

"I took her to the vet," said Mrs. Jameson. "She has all her shots now and a good health report." Greg and I were kneeling down with the puppy between us jumping up and licking our faces.

"She's good with kids," said Dad.

"Daddy, please let's keep her," I said.

"Let's call her Fudge," said Greg. Wow. I couldn't believe my little brother actually had a good idea.

"Well," said Dad, "sounds good to me."

So Fudge came home with us. Pepper hissed at her, banged her across the nose, then ignored her and went to sleep. I went to my computer:

To: Gran
Subject: Fudge
We got her and her name is Fudge! You know what? She's even housebroken. Here's a picture Daddy took. Isn't she the cutest thing you ever saw?

To: Adele
Subject: Re: Fudge
What a perfect way to start spring! Fudge looks darling. She's one lucky pup to get you and Gregory. Be sure to keep her safe on a leash, sweetie. Don't want her ever to run into the road again. Big hugs. Gran.

By April, the trees were a fuzzy green. Fudge ran around the yard barking at squirrels and getting muddy feet. A few days before Easter, Mom and I put together the baskets for the hospital kids. We filled them with Easter grass, chocolate eggs and bunnies and little candies. The next day, we

Eggs to Dye For

People used to get dyes from plants. You can, too. There are two ways of dyeing eggs: Boil them first, then cold-soak them in dyes; or boil them with the dye. * Boil eggs for 30 minutes or more with lots of onionskins; they'll turn a pale orange to light red. * Boil eggs with spinach leaves for pale green. * Soak hard-boiled eggs in grape juice; they'll turn lavender. * Boil eggs in tea for pale brown, in coffee for darker brown. * Boil eggs with beets or cranberries for lovely pinks and reds. * For a golden color, dissolve the spice turmeric in hot water and soak eggs. * To create patterns on boiled eggs, draw on the shells with wax crayons or wrap them in rubber bands before dyeing.

Go Fly a Kite

If it's windy enough to blow an umbrella inside out, don't try to fly a kite. But if a spring breeze is ruffling the branches of trees, it's probably perfect kite weather. What, you haven't got a kite? Check out the Internet—type "kites" in the search field of your browser or any good search engine. You'll find info on all kinds of affordable kites, stunt kites and kiting accessories—as well as safety tips for kite flyers (e.g., never fly over people, in thunderstorms, near trees or busy streets or power lines). Look for kite-flying events in your area. An awesome one is held every April in Miami. So get kiting—the sky's the limit!

Jellybean Bites

Each colorful bite delights with an assortment of jellybeans. They're perfect for Easter events or special springtime get-togethers. Makes 2 dozen Jellybean Bites.

I cup butter, softened
$1/2$ cup sugar
2 tablespoons water
I teaspoon vanilla extract
I egg yolk
$2^1/2$ cups flour
$1/2$ teaspoon baking soda
Parchment paper
I bag STARBURST® Brand Jellybeans

1. Cream the butter and sugar in a mixer until thoroughly combined.
2. Add the water, vanilla and egg yolk and mix thoroughly.
3. Add the dry ingredients. The dough should be firm. Refrigerate for half an hour.
4. Preheat the oven to 350°F.
5. Roll the dough into balls and place them on parchment paper–lined sheet pans. Bake for 5 minutes.
6. Remove from the oven and make an indentation on top of each cookie with thumb or spoon.
7. Place 3 STARBURST® Jellybeans in the indentation of each cookie, return to oven for 8–10 minutes, or until set and light brown.

took the baskets to the hospital, and even took Fudge along to visit the kids. We had permission. Mr. "Easter Bunny" Hansen was waiting for us, and we followed him into the kids' wing. It was the best thing.

When we got home, I sent an e-mail:

To: Gran
Subject: Success
The kids loved their baskets, but Fudge even better! She licked them all over and let them pet her. I hope I can take her back again this summer.

To: Adele
Subject: Re: Success
Delly, I'm so proud of you. And give Fudge a hug for me.

Gifts from Pressed Flowers

Make beautiful place or note cards using garden flowers. Pick small, flatish flowers like pansies, or grasses or small ferns. Place them between the pages of a big, heavy book protected with wax paper. Press down with a weight like cans of food or a brick. Leave for two or three weeks. When they are dry, experiment with different arrangements, then apply white glue to each flower's back and place on a card with tweezers. Put a clean piece of paper over the flower and press gently. Let dry.

Bunny Cookies

Makes 18 cookies.

1 (18-ounce) package refrigerated cookie dough

1 (16-ounce) container white frosting

Yellow and orange food coloring

1 bag **STARBURST® FUN SIZE®** Original Fruit Chews, unwrapped

1 bag **M&M'S®** Brand Chocolate Candies for Easter

1 tube or bag **M&M'S® MINIS®** Chocolate Candies

1. Preheat the oven to 350°F.
2. Roll the dough to $1/4$-inch thickness. Press out two sizes of cookies: 2-inch for bodies, 1-inch for heads. Arrange on a baking sheet, pressing bodies and heads together. Bake for 12–15 minutes and cool.
3. Divide the frosting into 3 bowls. Tint one with a few drops of yellow food coloring and one with orange. Frost each cookie orange, yellow or white.
4. Soften STARBURST® Fruit Chews in the microwave for 10 seconds. Mold into bunny ears and feet and press them into the cookies. Use M&M'S® Chocolate Candies for eyes, noses, mouths and elsewhere.
5. Soften one STARBURST® Fruit Chew in your hand (or for 5 seconds in the microwave) and divide into two equal parts. Shape half into a handle, half into a basket and mark weaving with a knife. Place basket on the cookie and fill with M&M'S® MINIS® Candies.
6. Soften one orange STARBURST® Fruit Chew for the carrot as shown and a green STARBURST® Fruit Chew cut into spiky fronds for its top.

EASTER

A Spring's Gift to Winter

The first flowers of spring grow from knobby things called bulbs. All winter the bulbs rest in the cold ground. Deep inside the bulb the flower is waiting. When the soil warms enough, the flower pushes upward through the earth to delight our eye. But here's the marvel: You can trick bulbs into blooming indoors in winter. Set bulbs in narrow-necked vases with the bottoms touching water. Soon roots will grow into the water and the flower will shoot up, filling your house with fragrance and color on dark winter days.

Bird's Nest Cookies

Makes 3 dozen cookies.

1 1/3 cups flaked coconut
2 sticks butter or margarine, softened
1/2 cup granulated sugar
1 large egg
1/2 teaspoon vanilla extract
2 cups all-purpose flour
3/4 teaspoon salt
1 bag M&M'S® Brand Speckled Milk Chocolate Eggs for Easter

1. Preheat the oven to 300°F. Spread coconut on nongreased cookie sheet. Toast in oven, stirring occasionally, until it turns light golden, about 25 minutes.
2. Remove coconut from cookie sheet and set aside.
3. Increase oven temperature to 350°F and lightly grease cookie sheets. In a large bowl, add butter and sugar and whip until light and fluffy. Beat in egg and vanilla.
4. In a medium bowl, combine flour and salt. Blend into creamed mixture.
5. Form dough into 1 1/4-inch balls. Roll heavily into toasted coconut. Place cookies 2 inches apart on cookie sheets. Make indentation with thumb in center of each cookie. Bake 12–14 minutes, or until golden brown.
6. Remove cookies and cool completely. Fill indentations with M&M'S® Speckled Eggs.

That afternoon Mom and I started dyeing eggs. Most of the eggs we boiled, but some we blew out so they were hollow. Yuck! "You could hang some of these blown-out eggs on your hat," Mom said. "What do you think?"

"Great idea," I said. I glued string to the eggs and hung them around the brim of the old straw hat that was going to be my Easter bonnet. Mom looked at me. "It needs something on top," she said.

I wondered what. I wanted it to be special, but I wasn't quite ready.

The next morning I woke up and saw something fluttering right outside my bedroom window. I slipped out of bed and tiptoed over. A bird's nest made of twigs and grass was wedged sort of behind the shutters. Inside were three pale blue eggs.

EASTER

The robins had been busy. And I'd been too busy to notice. Very quietly, I tiptoed to my computer:

To: Gran
Subject: Eggs
I just found out the robins built a nest right on my windowsill, and there are three little blue eggs in it!

To: Adele
Subject: Re: Eggs
How wonderful! Don't disturb them and you'll be able to see the babies hatch.

That gave me an idea. What my hat needed was a nest, right on top. I made it of twigs gathered from the backyard and hot glue, filled it with three dyed eggs and stuck it to the top of my hat. Ready for the Easter parade.

On Easter morning, we got up early and ate special sweet rolls that Mom makes. Then all of us, Fudge included, drove to the city. When we met Grandma at Rockefeller Center, she was wearing an amazing Easter bonnet in the shape of a baby lamb made of fleece and earrings from little colored plastic eggs.

"Grandma, you look beautiful!" I gave her a big fat hug.

She laughed. "Your hat is perfect," she said. "Let's join the parade."

The sun was shining and Fifth Avenue was totally crowded with all kinds of people, including TV guys and traffic cops. There were lots of dogs dressed up, too. Mom had some flowers in her hair instead of a hat, and Dad and Greg wore baseball caps. Fudge had a yellow kerchief. We walked and looked at all the hats. Some ladies wore huge straw ones with piles of flowers.

Bumble Bees

Makes 6 Bumble Bees.

Yellow construction paper
3 SNICKERS® Brand Creme Eggs
1 tube decorative yellow frosting
M&M'S® Brand Chocolate Candies for Easter

1. Cut 6 hearts from construction paper for the bee's wings (find a template at www.marsbrightideas.com).
2. Unwrap the SNICKERS® Creme Eggs and place both halves flat on a counter.
3. With the frosting, pipe lines over the eggs. For eyes, use M&M'S® Chocolate Candies.
4. Dot each wing with frosting, then press it underneath an egg, with one wing on either side of the egg.

Afterward, we drove to Gran's apartment.

It smelled delicious. She'd made an Italian Easter pie filled with all these cheeses, and roast leg of lamb, and finally a cake in the shape of a lamb. The cake tasted of vanilla, almonds, lemon and orange, and the white frosting was squiggly like wool. Late that night, I e-mailed Gran:

To: Gran
Subject: Thanks!
It was soooo good to see you. Your and my hats were the best. Dinner was deeeeeelicious and Greg says so, too. Please come see us soon. Please come before the eggs hatch and the babies fly away. You can stay in my room with me. Love, Delly

Gran came up just in time and stayed for a whole week. ∎

July 4th

Summer on the Lake

MORT TAPERT

 Reading Time 9–15 minutes

John hopes the Lius' summer sounds so great, his friend Ben will visit this year.

Dear Ben,

The best thing about summer, I just decided, is the fireworks on July 4th.

I start to think about the lake when it's March or April. It's still pretty foggy then in Washington State by the ocean. Thinking about the lake helps. My family has a cabin. A long time ago another family made it from trees they cut down nearby. My dad and uncles bought it a few years ago and added some rooms. They named it Wind in the Pines. It has a small front yard that goes down to the water, lots of pine trees and a little boathouse with a loft and its own wood stove. Best of all are lots of trails around the lake to other houses and great places to go like Rocky Hill, Fry Pan Point and Barefoot Bay. Every year I find new spots.

The way the cabin works is that three Liu families share it and every year we rotate which summer month the families get, but the time around 4th of July is for everybody. That's the high point of the summer for me. I sure hope you can come.

Being the July family means you are hosts for the 4th. Last year I got to be

Patriot Cake

Makes 24 servings.

2 (14-ounce) boxes pound cake mix (or your favorite cake mix, following the directions for pound cake)

2 (9 x 13-inch) nonstick cake pans

2 (16-ounce) containers white frosting

Blue food coloring

I bag red, white and blue M&M'S® Brand Milk or Peanut Chocolate Candies

1. Preheat the oven to 350°F. Prepare the pound cake batter according to the package directions. Pour the batter into the cake pans.
2. Bake the cakes for 35–40 minutes. Cool for 10 minutes, then remove and cool completely.
3. Cut one cake into two sizes, the first 5 x 7 inches and the second 7 x 9 inches.
4. Spoon $1/4$ of the frosting into a bowl. Add blue food coloring and blend. Spoon frosting into a resealable plastic bag. Set aside.
5. Frost the cake layers with the remaining white frosting. Beginning with the largest layer, stack them from largest to smallest.
6. Snip a corner of the resealable bag with the blue frosting. Mark off the top left corner of the cake with the blue frosting. Fill in the corner by squeezing on the remaining blue frosting and then spreading it smooth with the back of a spoon or a table knife.
7. Stars: Lace white M&M'S® Chocolate Candies in lines, covering the blue-frosted area. Stripes: lines with red M&M'S® Chocolate Candies.

boss of the boats. We have two canoes, a rowboat, two sailboats and an outboard. If many cousins come for the holiday, who gets what boat can be tricky. The outboard is only if you have a driver's license. It's one of the rules on the boathouse sign:

SIGN IN, SIGN OUT
WEAR LIFE VESTS
OUTBOARD FOR 16 AND OVER ONLY
[driver's license]
NO BATTLES
NO WATER CANNONS
RETURN _NOW_ AT THREE RINGS

The bell is for dinner and an emergency like a storm, which my little sister calls a "rumbly bumbly." It's a giant iron bell that will ring in your head for hours if someone clangs it when you're close. Once there was a fire in the kitchen and the adults were worried about where all the kids were. The bell rang three times over and over. By the time all our boats were off the lake, the fire was out—Dad did it with the big extinguisher that's kept in our front hallway. We had to cook over a campfire and use the hand pump for water until the kitchen was fixed. The older boys did the pumping and carried the pails. I was too young to pump; I helped look for firewood before dinner.

When you come, be sure it's for the 4th of July. It lasts all day with lots of events.

Caterpillar

Here's one insect that's welcome at any fun summer event.

Coconut (optional)

Green food coloring (optional)

2 multipack boxes M&M'S® Brand Cookie Ice Cream Sandwiches

1 bag red licorice

M&M'S® Brand Milk Chocolate Candies

Ready-made frosting

1. Color the coconut with green food coloring and spread it onto a serving tray. (This step is optional.)
2. Place 8 M&M'S® Ice Cream Sandwiches on top of the serving tray or green coconut. The sandwiches should be placed upright as shown in the photo.
3. Decorate with red licorice for legs and antennas.
4. Create a happy face on your caterpillar by sticking M&M'S® Chocolate Candies to the front of the caterpillar using ready-made frosting.

July 4th.

Everybody goes to the picnic and the fireworks. Everything starts with a boat parade, which is a big deal. Dad says it's nice and weird. Boats go slowly around one end of the lake and most of them are decorated. The first boat has a flute player dressed like a Revolutionary soldier (sort of) and a drummer. They play patriotic stuff. There's usually a "riot grrrl" boat, a vegetarian boat and a computer nerd boat. My relatives' boats are always goofy. Uncle Cho puts a tall stool in his canoe and tries to stay on top the whole way around, but usually comes home wet and laughing (you'll like him). Uncle Willy and his two sons dress like the British and have fake

Skipping Stones

The current world record for skips of a stone is 38. To get even a few skips you need flat water, a flat stone you can easily throw and a good arm. The trick is to make sure the stone spins a lot and travels low and fast. Hook your first finger around the stone, take your arm back low and throw so your arm stays parallel with the water, as if you were a baseball pitcher throwing sidearm. As your arm comes forward, let your wrist break. When you release the stone, it will spin out of your hand along your finger. The more you snap your wrist, the faster it will spin. If the stone flies low and flat, it will bounce lightly off the water again and again before sinking in a widening set of circular ripples.

Saving Good Bugs

Not all bugs are bad, of course. If a beautiful moth or butterfly gets inside the house, you want to help it get free. All you need is a good-sized clear drinking glass or empty jar and a piece of stiff cardboard, plastic or thin metal like the piece of aluminum painters hold to get clean edges. This temporary lid should overlap the container's edge by a good inch or so. Quietly and slowly approach the insect. Get the container ready. Capture the insect against a flat wall or window. Then slightly raise one edge enough to slide the lid under. Keep sliding while you gently hold down the container until the lid covers the whole container. Hold the lid in place. Take your prize outside, put the container right side up and watch a happy insect fly free again.

This technique also works for stinging insects like bees and wasps, but be careful!

July 4th.

fights with other boats. When the boats go past each house you're supposed to cheer, except for Uncle Willy's British boat. Then you get to boo like a maniac.

After the boat parade are all kinds of races and a family-only three-person volleyball tournament. In the Lius only my Uncle Willy and cousins Peter and Win play. Usually they do OK unless they are up against the Allen boys, who are trees and hardly ever lose. Then is a big picnic lunch at the Maplesons', a giant old house with a huge lawn at one end of the lake. Before the food are speeches and after is a softball game. My dad gave a speech one year. He

Signaling with Mirrors

When you go for a walk with a friend on a sunny day, take along a couple of small metal mirrors or very shiny pieces of metal with blunt edges. Stand on opposite sides of a big field or a valley with the sun between you. Practice holding the mirror so the sunlight bounces off the mirror toward your friend, who will see the mirror as a bright light. Now send signals by quickly tilting the mirror toward the ground then back to the position where it sends light to your friend. You can send short and long flashes of light and send the flashes slow or fast. Meet your friend in the middle and work out a code: one = yes, two = no, three = come here, lots of rapid flashes = watch out!

Ladybug Cupcakes

Makes 24 ladybugs.

1 box of your favorite cake mix

Cupcake liners

2 cupcake pans

1 (16-ounce) container vanilla frosting

Red food coloring

1 cup dark chocolate frosting

1 bag M&M'S® Brand Milk Chocolate Candies

12 black licorice laces cut into 48 pieces

2 bags of your favorite POP'ABLES™ Brand Candies

1. Prepare the cake mix according to the package directions.
2. Put liners into pans, fill each with $2/3$ cup batter.
3. Bake according to the package directions. Remove from the oven and cool.
4. Tint the vanilla frosting with the red food coloring and frost the cupcakes.
5. Spoon the chocolate frosting into a resealable plastic bag. Snip a small corner from the bag. Pipe a line of chocolate frosting down the center of each cupcake.
6. Pipe an oval of the chocolate frosting at one end of the line and decorate with red M&M'S® Chocolate Candies for eyes and the licorice for antennas. Dot the red portion with POP'ABLES™ Candies for the ladybugs' spots.

July 4th.

Thumb Puppets

Using fine-point felt-tip pens, draw bangs at the top of your thumbnail, little eyes, nose and mouth. Make a teeny head scarf from a 3-inch square of cloth (or a triangle 3 inches across). Tie it to fit. Or buy thumb-sized straw hats at the craft store. Wiggle your thumb and have conversations with your other thumb.

talked about how my grandparents came from China in the early 1950s and worked on a farm near the Skagit River. He said how friendly people were. Afterward a lot of our lake neighbors came over and shook his hand.

For the picnic, each family has to take something, which a group of ladies has lots of meetings about. Mom says they want to be sure there aren't 27 macaroni salads. She likes to take something that mixes fruit and meat, like tangerine beef or lemon chicken. It's fun to sit with new people each year, or some of them, anyway. That's the second rule of the 4th of July picnic: Eat with a different family. By now I feel like I know most of them. The desserts are on a separate table, all crowded together. Lots of them are red, white and blue. Why is it that cooks love to make desserts? Hey, I'm not complaining.

Star-Spangled Crispies

Makes 4–6 crispies.

1 (12-ounce) bag white chocolate chips
4 tablespoons margarine, melted
4 cups crispy rice cereal
1 bag M&M'S® Brand Chocolate Candies with red and blue candies separated out
Wax paper

1. Place white chocolate chips and margarine in a microwave-safe bowl.
2. Microwave at medium power for about 1 minute. Do not allow chocolate to burn.
3. Stir until mixture is smooth; combine with cereal and M&M'S® Chocolate Candies.
4. Drop onto wax paper–lined sheet pan to set.

July 4th.

Reunion Quilt Cake

Have the families attending a reunion bring one of these cakes. Then, on a big table, press all the cakes together to make a giant patchwork cake. Makes 1 (9-inch) cake.

Wax paper, parchment paper or foil
1 box of your favorite cake mix
1 (16-ounce) container vanilla or chocolate frosting
1 bag M&M'S® Brand Milk or Peanut Chocolate Candies

1. Preheat the oven to 350°F.
2. Butter a 9 x 9-inch cake pan and line the bottom.
3. Prepare the batter according to the package directions. Bake for 35 minutes. Remove and cool for 10 minutes. Lift the cake from the pan and cool completely before peeling the baking paper.
4. Frost top and sides of the cake. Decorate the top in a mosaic pattern with M&M'S® Chocolate Candies.

"Easier Than Pie" Pretzel Sticks

Makes 12 pretzel sticks.

Wax paper
1 cup M&M'S® Brand Milk Chocolate Candies
4 (1-ounce) squares semisweet chocolate
12 pretzel rods
4 (1-ounce) squares white chocolate

1. Line a baking sheet with wax paper; set aside.
2. Place M&M'S® Chocolate Candies in a shallow dish; set aside.
3. In top of a double boiler over hot water, melt 3 squares semisweet chocolate.
4. Remove from heat and dip 6 pretzel rods into chocolate, spooning chocolate to coat about $3/4$ of each pretzel.
5. Press into and sprinkle with M&M'S® Chocolate Candies; place on prepared baking sheet.
6. Refrigerate until chocolate is firm.
7. Repeat steps 3 through 6 with 3 squares white chocolate and remaining 6 pretzel rods.
8. Place remaining square semisweet chocolate and square white chocolate in separate small microwave-safe bowls and microwave for 30 seconds; stir. Repeat until chocolates are melted, stirring at 10-second intervals.
9. Drizzle white chocolate over semisweet chocolate–dipped pretzels; drizzle semisweet chocolate over white chocolate–dipped pretzels.
10. Sprinkle pretzels with any remaining M&M'S® Chocolate Candies.
11. Refrigerate 10 minutes, or until firm. Store tightly covered at room temperature.

61

July 4th.

The softball game happens in a field a farmer mows for us. It's not very serious, although I try to get hits and not make any errors. All the little kids get to bat. If they hit the ball, even if it goes two feet, they are always safe at first. The grown-ups even drop easy pop-ups and say "Whoops!" It's embarrassing. My cousins and I try to play ball, but we know it's just fooling around. If you come, we'll have a real game later.

The biggest thing you can do if you're a kid is be a fire usher when the fireworks go up. I was old enough for the first time last year. If you come on the 4th, I'll make sure you're included. After supper, which everyone has with their own families, we fire-usher kids go to the place where the firemen shoot the fireworks, in the baseball outfield. The firemen put up a fence all around it and park their trucks close. They give us all caps that say "Lake Ruckle Volunteer Fire Department" and show us the different kinds of fireworks they'll shoot up and how they'll do it.

That night, when the time came to start the fireworks, a fireman turned on a siren, which meant the dozen fire-usher kids had to tell everybody to move behind the safety line the firemen marked.

Then we stretched the safety rope and stood every few feet along it to keep people back, especially little kids. It was really dark. In the fireworks area across the field the light was red and the men moving inside the fence were just dark shapes and there was lots of smoke from the flares. It looked like everyone was running around, but my dad said it was as organized as a marching band. Fireworks look like big juice cans wrapped in paper with a

M&M'S MORES™ Cookie Logs

Makes 24 logs.

1³/₄ cups graham cracker crumbs

1 tablespoon sugar

6 tablespoons butter, melted

1¹/₂ cups sweetened shredded coconut (optional)

1 (14-ounce) can sweetened condensed milk

2 cups M&M'S® Brand Milk or Peanut Chocolate Candies

1¹/₂ cups mini marshmallows

¹/₂ bag DOVE® PROMISES® Milk Chocolate, unwrapped

1. Preheat the oven to 350°F.
2. Blend the graham cracker crumbs, sugar and butter in a large mixing bowl. Press the mixture into a buttered 9 x 13-inch baking pan.
3. Bake for 7 minutes.
4. Remove from the oven and sprinkle with the coconut, if desired.
5. Drizzle with the condensed milk and pop it back into the oven until bubbly and golden, about 10 minutes.
6. Remove and immediately cover with M&M'S® Chocolate Candies and marshmallows.
7. Put under a broiler for a few minutes, until the marshmallows turn a gooey golden brown.
8. Refrigerate until set, about 30 minutes. Cut into 1¹/₂ x 4¹/₂-inch bars and leave in pan.
9. Melt the DOVE® PROMISES® Chocolate for 15 seconds in the microwave or in a bowl placed on top of simmering water. Pour the chocolate into a resealable plastic bag. Snip a corner and drizzle the chocolate over the M&M'S MORES™ Cookie Logs.

The Perfect Knot

A good rainy-day learning is how to tie knots. The Queen of Knots is the bowline, pronounced BOW-lin. It is easy to tie and untie, strong, and is the loop knot for all time. Grasp the rope up from the end with one hand. Make a small over-

loop and hold it with your thumb—that's the rabbit hole. The end of the rope is the rabbit. With your other hand, push the end up the rabbit hole, around the piece you are holding (the tree) and back down the rabbit hole. Then pull tight. That's a bowline!

Nickname Fun

Do you like to think up nicknames for you and your friends? Your little brother? How about nicknaming local features, even the family car? The trick to a nickname is deciding what's the most important thing about this outcrop or that dog. A tree in the front yard can be "Mr. Barky." That big black rock by the field can be "Coal Head." The van can be "Magic." You get the idea. Now go out and name that shrub!

YOUR NAME HERE

---

long tube hanging out (that's the fuse). A fireman slides one down a fat pipe until it hits the bottom and hangs the fuse over. When the fire marshal says "Three, two, one, fire!" they light the fuse and step back fast. "Thunk!" goes the firework as it shoots straight up and smoke pours out of the pipe. Usually there are three or four launches at once. After a few seconds huge bright flowers in different colors pop open in the black sky and sometimes there are more pops. But the firemen don't even notice.

They are too busy making sure everything is all right and getting ready for the next launch. We just stood guard until the end, when they shot up a whole bunch of fireworks that made only white flashes and huge booms. You could hear the echoes in the mountains for a long time afterward. Let me know when you're coming!

Your friend,

John

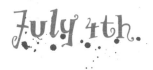

KUDOS® Brand Beach Pail

Makes 12 pails.

1 box **KUDOS® Brand Milk Chocolate Granola Bars Peanut Butter**, unwrapped

1 cup vanilla wafers

1 bag **DOVE® PROMISES® Milk Chocolate**, unwrapped

1 box ice cream wafer cups (available in grocery stores)

1 (16-ounce) container vanilla frosting

Yellow, red, blue and green food coloring

4 snack packs vanilla or chocolate pudding

1 bag **STARBURST® Brand Fruit Chews**, unwrapped

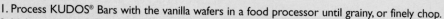

1. Process **KUDOS®** Bars with the vanilla wafers in a food processor until grainy, or finely chop.
2. Melt the **DOVE® PROMISES®** Chocolate in the microwave for 2 minutes. Stir until melted. Spoon 2–3 tablespoons into each ice cream wafer cup and spread it evenly around the bottom and sides with the back of a spoon. Set in the refrigerator for 5 minutes.
3. To frost the outside of the pails, tint the vanilla frosting with food coloring in a bold color. Spread on the outside of the wafer cups, completely covering them. Return to the refrigerator for 15 minutes to firm up.
4. Fill the wafer cups with layers of pudding and the **KUDOS®** mixture, finishing with 2 tablespoons of **KUDOS®** mixture. Set aside.
5. Make 12 groups of 4 **STARBURST®** Fruit Chews (each group should contain 4 **STARBURST®** Fruit Chews of the same color). Microwave 3 groups at a time for 5 seconds each, to soften. Mold these groups into shovels.
6. Microwave 12 randomly colored **STARBURST®** Fruit Chews for 5 seconds. Mold them into 6-inch strands and let them firm in an arch shape for handles.
7. Dab the edges of the handles with the frosting and place them on the top of each pail. Place the shovels decoratively next to the pails. Refrigerate until ready to serve.
8. Optional: Use ice cream instead of pudding. Let the ice cream soften at room temperature until you can easily scoop it into the wafer cups. Once filled, keep pails frozen until served.

Oh, Dear, Middle School Is Almost Here

NINDA DUMONT

 Reading Time 9–15 minutes

Joylee and Sadie are changing schools, and they're a little worried. Will it be hard? Or a chance to make new friends?

August 6

Summer's almost over and I'm not 100% all here. I'm partly melted! We've got a bad case of Baltimore "swamp-mug" as Grandmomma Waite used to call it. Also school starts in 3 weeks and I'm worried. My best friend Sadie & I have looked at lots of Web sites about middle school, because they help you about cliques and "budgeting" your time, and cleaning your locker.

Sadie won't be there, which stinks. Dad & Auntie Belle moved this summer so we could start buying our own house. Auntie B & Daddy are big sister & little brother like me & Lamar. When Mom died 5 years ago Auntie B came to help us, & ever since they're in cahoots about everything. I love her a lot.

This is the Most Important Thing that Sadie and I have to go through our whole lives so far & we won't even be

Brownie Gems

Little bites of brownie with extra candy inside—a great lunchbox surprise. Makes 24 Brownie Gems.

Mini cupcake pan
Mini cupcake liners
1 box of your favorite brownie mix
1 bag SNICKERS®, MILKY WAY® or 3 MUSKETEERS® Brand Miniatures

1. Preheat the oven to 350°F.
2. Line the cupcake pan with the liners.
3. Prepare the brownie mix according to the package directions.
4. Pour a little of the batter into each cupcake liner, then place unwrapped SNICKERS®, MILKY WAY® or 3 MUSKETEERS® Miniatures on top of the batter.
5. Pour additional batter into each cupcake liner, covering the Miniatures.
6. Bake for 20 minutes.

Number Cruncher Cookies

Do the math—these colorful numbers make a great (and tasty) teaching tool! Makes 8 equations.

- 1 (18-ounce) package refrigerated sugar cookie dough
- $1/3$ cup flour
- Number-shaped cookie cutters (You can also create your own number patterns.)
- 1 (16-ounce) container vanilla frosting
- Blue, red, green and yellow food coloring
- 1 bag M&M'S® Brand Milk or Peanut Chocolate Candies

1. Preheat the oven to 350°F.
2. Blend together the cookie dough and flour.
3. Roll to $1/4$-inch thickness on a lightly floured surface.
4. Press number shapes from the cookie dough with the cookie cutters (or patterns you've cut out). Don't forget to make minus, plus and equal signs!
5. Place on a cookie sheet and bake for 10–12 minutes.
6. While the cookies are cooling, divide the vanilla frosting among four small bowls and tint with the food coloring. Frost the numbers with the colored frosting. Dot the cookies with M&M'S® Chocolate Candies.
7. Display the cookies as equations.

together. Auntie B says even though Sadie will stay in our old neighborhood & we move $8^1/_2$ blocks doesn't mean anything in this day and age. "What if you lived on a farm like your great-grandparents?" is what she said.

Sadie & I will probably be on the phone or messaging all the time.

August 9

Auntie B says it's hard 2 B wise but I should try. She says I'll be "growing into" my feet before I know it & nobody will be looking at me anyway, because they will be scared about middle school too. "Just be yourself, Joylee, and you'll make new friends," she said. Auntie B makes the best of everything. She says artists & car mechanics are good at that too. Lamar doesn't care we moved, he's in 3rd grade & doesn't have to change schools.

August 10

Today was Super Swamp Day. But our whole family went to an African Dance Festival at the Inner Harbor! Sadie & her little brother Rowdy came too. Believe me, the name fits. We ate special African food. It's very spicy. Lucky for me they had LOTS of stuff without meat.

Then the drum music started & they danced like I do, only I used to have to make it up. I LOVE DRUMS. They

Make Sundae Faces Any Day

Make edible faces using ice cream as the base and all kinds of other stuff to create the features. Get the other stuff ready first, so the ice cream doesn't melt too much. Then put a scoop of ice cream into a dish and flatten with a big spoon. If you do a monster, use green ice cream and colored cereal. If you do a best friends sundae, put two scoops side by side, leaving room around each for hair. Work quickly so faces won't melt before you can admire your portrait! Then gobble 'em up!

Hair (Messy): broken shredded wheat cereal • crumbled brownies • peanut butter & shredded coconut • syrup

Hair (Neat): icing gel from tube • rows of round cereal • lined-up peanuts • chocolate whipped cream

Eyes: nuts • raisins • blueberries • round cereal

Ears: banana slices • cookie halves

Noses: cookie half • squirt of whipped cream • strawberry

Teeth: white chocolate bits • tiny marshmallows

Lips: maraschino cherries • strawberry slices

played djembe [JEM-BAY] and djun-djun [JOON-JOON] drums. Really cool. Men drummed & women danced. In Africa, men also dance. Everybody had on national dress costumes made of cotton in African designs. I know about African art because Dad and Auntie Belle buy African carvings or a wall hanging every year at the art festival.

The best thing was they asked if any girls wanted to learn African dancing. Sadie & I jumped up with our hands in the air and we got chosen with 10 others. One little girl was about 3. We took off our shoes and learned how to stamp & move up & back & shake our elbows & shoulders in time to the drum. It was sooooo hot. I wonder if Africa is this hot. We danced about 15 minutes & everybody clapped and whistled. There

Auntie Belle's 10 Friendship Tips

1 Always be yourself—don't be fake.

2 Brush your teeth & put on a smile in the morning.

3 Be honest.

4 Listen! You might learn something.

5 Share with others.

6 Learn to keep a secret.

7 Be true to your friends and you will always have them.

8 Have a good sense of humor.

9 Be friends with kids you admire.

10 Say something nice or nothing at all.

back to school

Train Your Brain— Study Tips

- Brains don't run on hot air. Eat breakfast!
- Pay attention, don't get attention. Listen in class.
- Every new word deserves ink. Write facts, words & questions in a notebook.
- Write down assignments, every word. No shortcuts!
- Use down time during the day to read, write or do a math problem. You might be through homework before school is out.
- Get Team Study Spirit! Have a study partner who helps you with one subject & whom you can help with another.
- Stiff necks not allowed! Put books & papers where you can read & write comfortably.
- Yaawwwwwn at home, not in school! Relax between classes. Stretch & roll your shoulders & wiggle your feet.
- Snackin' time! Everybody feels a little pooped about 3 or 4 in the afternoon. Just don't spoil your appetite for supper.

Pennant Cookies

Great for the bake sale!

1 (18-ounce) package sugar cookie dough
Craft sticks
1 (16-ounce) container white frosting
Food coloring
1 bag **M&M'S® Brand Milk Chocolate Candies**

1. Roll out sugar cookie dough and cut out triangle shapes.
2. Add a craft stick to the back of each cookie and adhere with a small ball of additional cookie dough.
3. Bake according to package directions and let cool.
4. Tint frosting to school colors in separate bowls, frost cookies and decorate with M&M'S® Chocolate Candies.

were lots of tourists watching. Lamar got Dad to buy him a braided cord with a cowrie shell. Cowrie shells used to be money in Africa. Wouldn't it be fun to pay for stuff with cowrie shells? Like a coconut ice would be 15 cowrie shells!

August 12

Back to serious stuff. One thing about being in the middle of Baltimore is I can walk to my new school. Dad or Auntie B used to drive me to school every morning until spring. Then they let me walk with Sadie, but Lamar still had to go in the car since I am a "flibbertigibbet" who forgets to watch out for him. The flibbertigibbet

is the artist in me, which is what I'll be when I grow up. And a poet. Sadie & I make up stuff while we're walking.

I hope I have somebody good to walk with.

August 15

We are having a party next week! It was Sadie's idea. Her mom called around her "network" and Auntie B did too, and they luckily found out they knew 8 parents of kids in my new school. So those kids (I hope I like them) & our friends from elementary will come to an Ice Cream Social in our new backyard!

Everybody is bringing what they like on ice cream or frozen yogurt (my new thing). Sadie & I are practicing an Old Friends New Friends song and we'll dance to African music.

Lamar promised 2 B good & not B disgusting and chew with his mouth open. He said since it was an ice cream party he would chill. Brothers!

August 24

We had the Ice Cream Social yesterday and it was so great. I wish Daddy could have been there, but he had to work.

I liked everybody except one girl who was stuck-up. Auntie B says she's probably shy. Some mother & grandmother chaperones came too. 13 kids came from our elementary class, plus us and 9 kids (2 boys) from my new middle school.

Sadie thought of a surprise—every kid brought plants or bulbs for a Friends Garden in our yard! We put it all in the shade until Dad & I could plant & water them. Lamar kept the secret too. He & Dad loosened the dirt for my Friends

SNICKERS® Apples

Bet the teacher has never gotten an apple like this sweet treat! Makes 6 apples.

6 apples, washed and patted dry
6 craft sticks
2 bags soft caramels, unwrapped
2 tablespoons water
1 bag DOVE® PROMISES® Milk Chocolate, unwrapped
1 bag SNICKERS® Brand Miniatures, unwrapped
Wax paper

1. Press the craft sticks into the tops of the apples.
2. Melt the caramels with water in a 4-cup microwave-safe glass measuring cup for 1–2 minutes in the microwave. Stir occasionally until smooth.
3. Dip the apples into the caramels, rolling each apple to cover it completely. Set them on the wax paper and refrigerate for 10 minutes.
4. Melt the DOVE® PROMISES® Chocolate in the microwave for 15 seconds. Stir until smooth.
5. Roughly chop the SNICKERS® Miniatures.
6. Dip the chilled apples into the melted chocolate and immediately roll them in the chopped SNICKERS® Miniatures, covering each apple entirely.

Garden the day before yesterday while Auntie Belle & I went out grocery shopping. I got 22 different plants! The names & the kids' names we wrote on craft sticks with a felt pen. We have to mulch everything before the winter.

Who knows, we might get a big snow again! The bulbs won't come up until spring, and the annual flowers have to be planted again next year but that's OK.

I got a Daffodil bulb from Sadie, a Marigold from Isaac, a Tulip bulb from Abe,

Spirit Flags

Celebrate diversity and learn about our world's nationalities with easy-to-make (and yummy) flags.

**Graham crackers
1 (16-ounce) container white frosting
1 bag M&M'S® Brand Milk Chocolate Candies**

1. Frost graham crackers with white frosting.
2. Decorate with a variety of different-colored M&M'S® Chocolate Candies.

For flags of your heritage, consult an encyclopedia or go to http://education.yahoo.com/reference/factbook/flags/a.html.

Stop & Go Brownies

These bright treats will make safety fun! Makes 24 brownies.

**1 box of your favorite brownie mix
Wax paper, parchment paper or foil
1 (16-ounce) container vanilla frosting
Yellow food coloring
2 bags M&M'S® Brand Milk or Peanut Chocolate Candies**

1. Prepare the brownie batter according to the directions for cake-style brownies found on the box. Evenly spread the batter in a 9 x 13-inch baking pan lined with wax paper.
2. Bake and cool brownies completely. Remove the brownies from the pan, then remove the wax paper.
3. If desired, tint vanilla frosting with yellow food coloring to the desired shade. Spread frosting evenly on top of the brownies. Cut into 1 x 2-inch rectangles.
4. Set aside 24 green, 24 yellow and 24 red M&M'S® Chocolate Candies. Dot each brownie rectangle like a traffic light with one red, one yellow and one green M&M'S® Chocolate Candy.

Talking Flowers

People had a "flower language" 150 years ago. They gave each other bouquets that said a lot without speaking out loud. You could do that, too, or use flower names as code language in notes or e-mails.

Amaryllis = "You're beautiful, but I'm shy."

Apple blossom = "I like you best."

Camellia = "Thank you!"

Carnation = "I love you truly."

White Chrysanthemum = "This is the truth."

Four-Leaf Clover = "Be mine."

Red Daisy = "You're beautiful even if you don't know it."

Wild Daisy = "I'll think about it."

Dandelion = "I'm flirting with you!"

Fern = "You are fascinating & sincere."

Holly = "Did you forget me?"

Iris = "I've got a message for you."

Ivy = "I'll be true to you."

Lily of the Valley = "I'm happy again!"

Oak Leaves = "We will be brave!"

Parsley = "I feel silly."

Purple Pansy = "I'm thinking about you."

Red Rose = "I love you."

White Rose = "I won't tell."

Sweet Pea = "Let's get together."

Violet = "I'm your faithful friend."

Zinnia = "I'm sad since you went away."

a striped Hosta plant from Gemma, a Lavender from Chadia, a dark purple grass with berries from Sophie, a teeny Mustard greens plant from Roberto which he dug out of his mom's garden, a Queen Anne's Lace from Turner (that's a girl at my new school), a Fern from Greeley, plus lots more. I will write thank-you notes TOMORROW. Auntie B said I couldn't "procrastinate."

It was the best party I ever went to. We had vanilla, French vanilla, strawberry and chocolate ice cream & vanilla frozen yogurt. One kid brought frozen vanilla soy milk in a cooler. It was even better than the yogurt! One thing we did was make sundae faces, with scoops of ice cream for heads, and other things for eyes, noses, mouths & hair.

After we ate everybody sat down and Sadie & I put a drum CD on and we danced about 1 minute before everybody was dancing too. Instead of worrying

Squabbler Cupcakes

Makes 18 cupcakes.

1 (18.5-ounce) box favorite cake mix
Cupcake liners
Cupcake pan
1 (16-ounce) container white frosting
Red, green, blue and yellow food coloring
Wide craft sticks
Decorative candy: STARBURST® Brand
Original Fruit Chews cut in half, M&M'S®
Brand Milk or Peanut Chocolate Candies and POP'ABLES™ Brand Candies

1. Prepare the cake batter according to the package directions.
2. Line the cupcake pan with the cupcake liners.
3. Pour $1/2$ cup of batter into each cupcake liner. Bake for 18–20 minutes.
4. While the cupcakes are cooling, prepare the decorations. Divide the frosting among 4 small bowls. Tint each bowl with a shade of food coloring. Put the STARBURST® Fruit Chews and M&M'S® Chocolate Candies into the bowls and place them on a table where children can easily reach them.
5. Let them frost the cupcakes with the craft sticks. Decorate the cupcakes like funny faces, using softened and molded pieces of STARBURST® Fruit Chews, M&M'S® Chocolate Candies and POP'ABLES™ Candies.

about Lamar I should have locked my dog Emitte in my room because he ran around barking & begging for ice cream all afternoon! Lamar pretended to be drumming on the plastic bucket Dad uses to haul plant-food water. I know I made a lot of friends. The grown-ups took lots of pictures.

September 15

Middle School rules! I told Auntie Belle I'm pretty sure I am popular. She told me not to let it go to my head. "Just be yourself, Joylee"—like always. Daddy said we're going to have a grill party soon for my whole class. So nobody feels left out, because the Ice Cream Social is famous at school.

Whenever I wish Sadie was with me, I touch the hem of my skirt. She does the same when she thinks about me. We had the brilliant idea of using a laundry pen to put our names & a heart on the inside hems of our school uniform skirts (blue plaid &

Make a Vocabulary Notebook

How many English words do you think there are? Not counting scientific words, well over 500,000. People use only 1,000 or 2,000 words for everyday talking or writing. (Most adults think kids have only ten words they use: "no," "why," "yeah," "uh," "like," "you know.") The right words help you say more. Learn more words and put them in your brain forever, like a word bank. They will help you say what you mean!

One way to learn more words is with a vocabulary notebook, on paper or on your computer.

To start, give each letter at least two pages. Copy words from books or what you read online, or cut out words and sentences from the newspaper. When you hear a new word, get help spelling it correctly. In your notebook, write the new word's meaning and how it is pronounced. Write a poem about a word that sounds cool.

Read dictionaries—they can be fun and really interesting. Try "R"—look up "ragtag," "rapscallion" and "rigmarole." Prefer "P"? Look up "perky," "persnickety" and "pipkin." Add words weekly—and use them!

You're a Star Cookies

A sweet reward for any special teacher or kid who deserves a boost! Makes 15 stars.

1 (18-ounce) roll refrigerated sugar cookie dough
$1/3$ cup flour
Star-shaped cookie cutter
Tube of colored decorative frosting, such as blue or yellow
1 bag M&M'S® Brand Milk or Peanut Chocolate Candies or M&M'S® MINIS® Milk Chocolate Candies MEGA TUBE®

1. Preheat the oven to 350°F.
2. Blend the cookie dough and flour together.
3. Roll to $1/4$-inch thickness on a lightly floured surface.
4. Press star shapes from the cookie dough with the cookie cutter.
5. Bake them on a cookie sheet for 12–14 minutes.
6. Once cooled, use the frosting to attach M&M'S® Chocolate Candies or M&M'S® MINIS® Candies around the outside edges of the cookies. Write special messages on the cookies, like "You're a Star."

plain blue for me, and maroon plaid & plain maroon for Sadie). All we have to do is touch our hems & we feel together. She loves her new school too, but even though she has new friends, Sadie & I will be best friends forever. I can just tell. ■

HALLOWEEN

The Monster Bash

KATHY KINGSLEY

 Reading Time 9–15 minutes

How one family in the Southwest combines a party and a town celebration to make a very festive Halloween.

Everybody always tells us our annual Halloween party is special. The day my mother and I send out the invitations, I can barely sit still. She has to do the addresses—I am so jumpy, I make too many mistakes. Over the years, our party has grown from family and friends to dozens of families—Mom says 130 people came last year. It starts on a Sunday afternoon when everyone arrives at the town square for a costume parade and a group photo. Later they all come to our backyard for an outdoor supper. I love the whole day, but I love remembering it even more.

Our planning has to begin early, in September. I get to help think about what will happen when everyone comes to our backyard. My mother and her two sisters, Rosa and María, keep getting stuff from magazines and ideas from the Internet. We get together and think about ideas for the many backyard stations that we have to set up, for things like applying tattoos and mask decorating and cookie break, and talk about what worked well last time and what was

Black Cat Cupcakes
Makes 24 cupcakes.

- 24 cupcake liners
- 2 (12-cup) cupcake pans
- 1 box chocolate cake mix
- 1 bag TWIX® Brand FUN SIZE® Cookie Bars
- 2 (16-ounce) containers chocolate frosting
- 1 bag SKITTLES® Brand Bite Size Candies
- 1 bag black or red licorice laces

1. Preheat the oven to the recommended temperature. Place the cupcake liners in the cupcake pans.
2. Prepare the cake batter according to the package directions.
3. Chop 12 TWIX® Cookie Bars and set aside.
4. Pour $1/8$ cup of the batter into each cupcake liner.
5. Top with a generous tablespoon of chopped TWIX® Cookie Bars and finish with a final layer of $1/4$ cup of batter.
6. Bake until a toothpick inserted into the cupcake is clean when removed. Cool cupcakes completely before frosting.
7. Frost each cupcake, use SKITTLES® Bite Size Candies for eyes and nose, black and red licorice cut into strips for whiskers and in half diagonally for ears.

a flop. One thing I remember from last year was making Green Goopy Goo, which is stretchy, rubbery stuff that's a lot of fun to squish and pull. What's so cool is that it's made of glue, water, food coloring and borax cleaning powder.

Of course, costumes are a big deal. What I like is that some people wear what they think they are, some wear what they want to be and most people just wear something for fun. In Christina's case, my little sister, her costumes always tend to be built around tutus left over from her most recent ballet recital. She'll always rush to

say that she is not simply a ballerina but a "spring flower" or some other crazy thing. The last couple of years I've tried to convince her that she should dress in something different, but she is really stubborn for a six-year-old.

One of my favorite costumes started as a black dress that my mom made on the sewing machine. With some wire, black crepe paper and yellow and white construction-paper cutouts, I was a really good monarch butterfly, if I may say so. The idea came from Aunt María. She said that in Mexico, where she grew up, they didn't

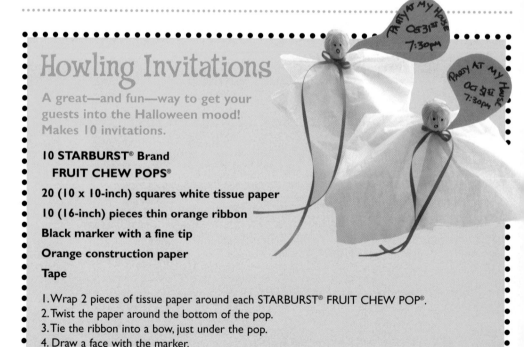

Howling Invitations

A great—and fun—way to get your guests into the Halloween mood! Makes 10 invitations.

10 STARBURST® Brand
FRUIT CHEW POPS®

20 (10 x 10-inch) squares white tissue paper

10 (16-inch) pieces thin orange ribbon

Black marker with a fine tip

Orange construction paper

Tape

1. Wrap 2 pieces of tissue paper around each STARBURST® FRUIT CHEW POP®.
2. Twist the paper around the bottom of the pop.
3. Tie the ribbon into a bow, just under the pop.
4. Draw a face with the marker.
5. Cut the orange construction paper into a small oval.
6. Write the party details on the paper and attach it to the ghost with tape.

HALLOWEEN

Guess Ghoul Game

For a party, write the names of characters from movies or books on index cards. (For younger kids use Halloween characters like witch, mummy, ghost.) Pin cards to the guests' backs when they arrive, so they can see the names on the other players' backs but not the names on their own. Guests have to figure out whose names are pinned on their backs by asking questions about those people or characters. When everybody has guessed their name, it's treat time.

celebrate Halloween, but something like it called All Souls' Day that begins on October 31 and runs for three days. The monarch butterflies are an important part of their celebration, because in autumn the butterflies that spent the summer in the north fly south to have a nice winter in the forests. She has a way of saying it, which I wrote down: "The graceful butterflies embroider the air with their orange and black finery as they glide to their roosting places in the trees." In one forest near her house she said there were over 30 million butterflies!

Then there was the year my older cousin Peter decided he was too old to take part in dressing up and made no preparations at all. On the day of the party he started having second thoughts and by the time it was about to begin he decided he just had to be in the costume parade. He

Halloween Riddles

What kind of music do ghosts listen to?
A: Sheet music.

How do monsters tell their future?
A: They read their horrorscope.

Why did Dracula go to the orthodontist?
A: To improve his bite.

What kind of mistakes do spooks make?
A: Boo-boos.

Why do mummies make good spies?
A: They're good at keeping things under wraps.

How does a witch tell time?
A: She looks at her witch watch.

decided a white sheet with eyeholes cut out wasn't good enough. His big sister got into the act. She found a really old suit in the attic. It had a shirt with a high collar, a vest and a fun black hat with a little brim and round top. By the time she finished giving him bushy gray sideburns and gray hair, Peter looked just like some old president. He was the hit of the parade! The thought of his trying to act all grown up and serious still makes me LOL.

As the day of the party gets closer, so does our annual trip to the pumpkin patch. No Halloween party is complete without lots of good jack-o'-lanterns. In the area where we live in New Mexico, many pumpkins grow, and the search for the perfect ones to carve can take my family a whole afternoon. We drive to a farm at the foot of the mountains. Every October, a chunk of the farm is a pick-your-own pumpkin patch. I love seeing the

Goblin Bars
Makes 9 bars.

- I package brownie mix
- I bag DOVE® PROMISES® Milk or Dark Chocolate
- I bag SNICKERS® Brand FUN SIZE® Bars
- I bag M&M'S® Brand Milk Chocolate Candies for Halloween

1. Prepare the brownie mix according to the package directions for an 8 x 8-inch pan. Bake and cool slightly.
2. Place the DOVE® PROMISES® Chocolate in a mixing bowl over a pot of simmering water.
3. Stir the chocolate as it melts. When it is shiny and smooth, turn off the heat. Pour half of the chocolate over the top of the brownies and set aside the remaining half.
4. Sprinkle with 3/4 cup chopped SNICKERS® FUN SIZE® Bars and I cup M&M'S® Chocolate Candies.
5. Drizzle remaining DOVE® PROMISES® Chocolate on top. Cool completely.

Treat Bag

To make a cat treat bag, draw the side view of a cat's body with a black paint marker onto the front of a solid-color paper bag, such as white or orange, with handles. Cut out the front view of a cat head from black crafts foam. Glue it to the side of the bag at the top. Glue on eyes and a nose cut from colored crafts foam. Use black chenille pipe cleaners for whiskers and a tail. Attach the tail to the opposite side.

Ghoulish Party Pizza Cookie

This big, chocolatey cookie treat will be the hit of the party. Makes 12 servings.

1 (18-ounce) package refrigerated
  sugar cookie dough
$1/8$ cup flour
$1/3$ cup mini marshmallows
$1/2$ cup roughly chopped SNICKERS®
  Brand FUN SIZE® Bars
1 cup M&M'S® Brand Chocolate Candies
  for Halloween

1. Preheat the oven to 350°F.
2. On a lightly floured surface, knead the cookie
   dough into a ball. Place the ball on a cookie
   sheet and roll into a 12-inch circle, flouring the
   rolling pin as needed. Score the dough into
   "pizza" wedges, using the tip of a knife. Bake
   for 15 minutes.
3. Remove and top with the mini marshmallows,
   SNICKERS® FUN SIZE® Bars and M&M'S®
   Chocolate Candies. Return to the oven
   and bake for 7 minutes longer, simply to
   soften candies.
4. To serve, cut into wedges.

distant fields kind of glow orange as our car approaches. It is just the thing to put you in a Halloween mood. My friend Shane usually comes with us. We call him the "Pumpkin Picasso," because he always works so hard to make his carved pumpkin different and interesting every year.

After we get home with our prizes, we gather on our front porch and the task of turning them into jack-o'-lanterns begins. Everyone gets to work. Mostly there are faces with weird eyes and jagged toothy grins and maybe a fang or two. "Carve away," my dad encourages us. "We want these pumpkins to talk!" That's no problem for Shane. One year he carved a coyote howling in front of a full moon, and another time it was a witch with her cat on a broom. When you go trick-or-treating at his pueblo on Halloween night, the place glows with the coolest jack-o'-lanterns you ever saw.

Food is a big part of our celebration and my mother and aunts prepare it all. They are known as great cooks and don't mind it one bit. One of Mama's specialties is a sauce of chocolate and chile. It's called a *mole* (moe-lay). She adds chicken to it for the Halloween party, stirring it and stirring it again. The *mole* fills the house with a wonderful smell. I always try to sneak a taste of the sauce when she's not looking. "*Espérense*" (wait), she says when she catches me. Aunts Rosa and María make tamales, which are corn husks

Wrap the Mummy

Divide the guests into teams of two. Give each team a roll of toilet paper. On each team, one person wraps and the other is wrapped. The entire roll of toilet paper must be used. Whoever wraps the mummy fastest wins.

Candy Cauldrons

Kids can make and decorate their own mini Candy Cauldrons—great for Halloween party favors.

Black paper cups (or paint any paper cup black with nontoxic paint)

Nontoxic black and white paint

Plastic spiders

White glue

Hole punch

Black pipe cleaners

Cotton balls

An assortment of M&M'S®, SNICKERS®, MILKY WAY®, TWIX®, 3 MUSKETEERS®, SKITTLES® and STARBURST® Brand FUN SIZE® Candies

1. Use white paint to paint a spider's web onto the cup.
2. Glue on a spider for an authentic look.
3. Use a hole punch on the sides of the cup to secure the pipe cleaner handle.
4. Apply white glue to the rim of the cauldron and arrange cotton balls.
5. Repeat the above steps to create as many cauldrons as desired.
6. Fill with an assortment of FUN SIZE® candies.

stuffed with cornmeal dough and different filling, then they are steamed. Preparing tamales is a lot of work and my aunts only make them for big occasions. Our Halloween party is one of those times and it makes our guests feel very special.

In keeping with the Halloween theme, our menu has items like ghost-shaped cheese sandwiches, pumpkin-shaped pasta in cheese sauce and my personal favorite, Monster Toes (mini hotdogs in biscuit dough, with the franks sticking out and dipped in ketchup). I also love the mini corn muffins and the Spider Punch floating with blobs of orange sherbet and "black widows" that have marshmallow bodies and licorice legs.

When I wake on the morning of the party, I'm always anxious. Even though I have plenty of chores to

Bats

So easy to make, all your little goblins can help you go batty!

Black construction paper

Bat template

Scissors

An assortment of M&M'S®, SNICKERS®, MILKY WAY®, TWIX®, 3 MUSKETEERS®, SKITTLES® and STARBURST® Brand FUN SIZE® Candies

Double-stick tape

1 bag M&M'S® Brand Milk Chocolate Candies for Halloween

1. Trace the bat templates onto black construction paper. Cut out the shapes.
2. Adhere an assortment of FUN SIZE® Candies to the bat shapes, using double-stick tape.
3. For eyes, adhere orange M&M'S® Chocolate Candies, using double-stick tape.

Spooky Tales

Let's be spooky.
  Let's have fun
And talk of spells
  and ghostly ones
Haunted houses,
  creaking bones
Foggy evenings,
  zombie moans

Let's give ourselves
  a scare, let's do
With a tale
  of bubbling brew
Sobbing ghouls,
  winds that howl
Wicked vampires
  on the prowl

Let's be spooky
  in the night
Have a witch
  switch off the lig
Let's imagine
  ghostly scenes
Why, you ask?
  It's Halloween!

HALLOWEEN

Phantom Ghost

Gather the family for some creative fun.

White balloon
Black permanent marker
Empty one-gallon plastic milk container
Double-stick tape
Clear cellophane
White ribbon
An assortment of M&M'S®, SNICKERS®,
 MILKY WAY®, TWIX®, 3 MUSKETEERS®, SKITTLES®
 and STARBURST® Brand FUN SIZE® Candies

1. Draw a ghost face on the balloon with a black permanent marker.
2. Cut a large hole (big enough for hands) in the front of the milk container.
3. Secure the balloon on top of the milk container with double-stick tape.
4. Cover the balloon and milk container with clear cellophane and secure with double-stick tape.
5. Tie a white ribbon around the neck of the Phantom Ghost.
6. Fill Phantom Ghost with an assortment of FUN SIZE® Candies.
7. Surprise a friend by leaving the Phantom Ghost on his or her doorstep.

keep me busy, I keep checking the clock until it's finally time to get ready for the costume parade. The edges of the town square are full of people watching and applauding all the costumed figures. The parade comes to a rest right in our backyard, which is only a block away. The marchers all gather for group photos taken by many different people (last year our picture made it into the local newspaper), and then everyone can enjoy all the activities that we've planned and the tables filled with festive food. If the neighborhood musician, Mr. O'Leary, is at our party, he'll strum his guitar and sing all sorts of tunes. Sometimes my dad will join him on the bongo drums. A basket filled with tambourines and maracas is nearby for anyone else who wants to join in. My aunts and uncles have fun dancing.

At the end of the party, the children gather for the piñata. A piñata is a wire frame covered with papier-mâché and frilly colored crepe paper. They come in all

More Halloween Riddles

When is it bad luck to meet a black cat?
A: When you're a mouse.

What do skeletons say before dining?
A: Bone appetite.

What do you get when you cross a snowman and a vampire?
A: Frostbite.

How do you mend a broken jack-o'-lantern?
A: With a pumpkin patch!

Jack-o'-Lantern Brownies

Pumpkin-shaped treats with a big brownie taste. Makes 12 brownies.

Parchment paper

1 box (for 9 x 13-inch pan) brownie mix

1 (16-ounce) container white frosting

Orange food coloring

1 bag M&M'S® Brand Milk Chocolate Candies for Halloween

1. With parchment paper, line the bottom only of a 9-inch round baking pan.
2. Prepare the brownie mix and bake according to the package directions.
3. Cool completely, then unmold brownies and place on a platter.
4. Add orange food coloring to the white frosting and frost the brownies.
5. Use black M&M'S® Chocolate Candies for Jack-o'-Lantern's eyes, nose and mouth. Completely cover the rest of the Jack-o'-Lantern in a pattern with orange M&M'S® Chocolate Candies.

shapes and sizes and the center is filled with small candies and some-times little toys. In years past, we've made piñatas in the shapes of a star-burst, a fat witch and a smiling ghost. My dad strings the piñata from a tree branch over the patio and raises and lowers it with a rope. The children take turns being blindfolded. They swing at the piñata with a stick. Finally, after a really big whack (usual-ly delivered by cousin Peter), the piñata bursts open, scattering candy everywhere. The children scamper to pick up the sweets and the search continues by flashlight until the very last piece is found.

I'm sad when the day ends, but Shane always reminds me that there's still a Halloween party at school and a night of trick-or-treating ahead of us. In my neighborhood, the adobe hous-es are built close together, so you can cover a lot of territory in a short time and fill your candy bag to the brim. I love going to the O'Learys' house on Halloween, because you have to walk through their yard full of real-looking snakes, old bones, bats and cobwebs on the way to the front door. Then Mrs. O'Leary offers us a choice—col-orful plastic worms from a big bowl or candy from another. I always choose the worms.

I know that there are other fun holidays to look forward to after Halloween ends (Christmas and Valentine's Day aren't so bad), but I always find myself counting the days until my mother and I can send out the invitations to our next Halloween party. ◼

M&M'S® MINIS® Night Owls

Cut your own **Night Owl** shapes out of cookie dough, then get the whole family in on the decorating fun! Makes 8 owls.

**Owl template (available at
  www.marsbrightideas.com)
1 (18-ounce) package sugar cookie dough
1 (16-ounce) container chocolate frosting
1 (16-ounce) container white frosting
1 bag M&M'S® MINIS® Milk Chocolate
  Candies for Halloween**

1. Create beautiful Night Owls by cutting out an owl shape from cookie dough and baking according to the package directions.
2. Decorate with chocolate and white frosting.
3. Detail the Night Owls with brown ears, yellow eyes, orange wings and a red tail using M&M'S® MINIS® Candies.

An Easy Fun Piñata

You need a balloon, string, papier-mâché mixture and crepe paper. Simply smooth a couple of layers of papier-mâché over an inflated balloon. Between layers, wrap some string around the globe and leave the ends for tying. To dry, balance it on a widemouthed glass. Cut a trap door and fill the cavity with candy, confetti and other treats like small toys, then tape the door shut. Decorate with strips of crepe paper. Make into a pumpkin, monster, eyeball or even a full moon with bats.

RECIPE INDEX

For a recipe or to use a specific candy, you've come to the right place!

Color Key: Christmas   Valentine's Day   Easter   July 4th   Back to School   Halloween

CREDITS

Christmas

Nancy Holyoke is the author of six books in the American Girl Library, including *Oops! A Manners Guide for Girls* and *A Smart Girl's Guide to Boys*. She was the founding editor of *American Girl* magazine. She lives in Madison, Wisconsin, with her husband and 15-year-old son.

Valentine's Day

Peter and **Connie Roop** have written 60 children's books together, fiction and nonfiction, and made hundreds of presentations to student and teacher groups. Seven of their books are Reading Rainbow books, including *Keep the Lights Burning, Abbie*. Peter is a past Wisconsin State Teacher of the Year; Connie is a high school environmental science teacher.

Easter

Andrea DiNoto is the author of books and articles on numerous subjects, with emphasis on the decorative arts, design and collecting. Her most recent book (coauthored with David Winter), *The Pressed Plant: "The Art of Botanical Specimens, Nature Prints, and Sun Pictures,"* was named American Horticultural Society Book of the Year. She was a contributing editor of *Connoisseur*.

July 4th

Mort Tapert is a writer and editor with a close connection to children on lakes. He taught swimming as a young man, helped run a sailing school and was Lake Michigan East Coast sailing champion in 1969. He lives in New York City and Millerton, New York, where lakes are termed ponds.

Back to School

Ninda Dumont makes her living doing books for girls, and also kitchen antiques books (the latest, fifth edition, is 893 pages). She is embarking on a series of mysteries that are located in her mid-19th-century neighborhood in Baltimore.

Halloween

Kathy Kingsley has written five cookbooks, including *Chocolate Cakes*, selected by Julia Child as one of the 10 best cookbooks of 1993. She was the food editor of *Vegetarian Times* for five years and has produced cookbook series for *Food and Wine* and *Reader's Digest*. She also writes for children and contributes to *Family Fun* magazine. She lives in Connecticut with her husband and two daughters.

Publisher
Joan Montgomery

Associate Publisher
Peter Zegras

Editorial Director
Tom Parrett

Designers
KC Witherell, Aimee Zaleski

Photography
Geoffrey Thomas

Illustration
Gary Halgren

Copy Editor
Arlene Bouras

Production Director
Rose Sullivan

Chief Technical Officer
Sam Bone

The Magazine Works, Inc.
260 Harbor Road
Southport, CT 06890